After Jack

Garry Thomas Morse

Talonbooks

Talonbooks
Box 2076, Vancouver, British Columbia, Canada V6B 3S3
www.talonbooks.com

Typeset in Adobe Garamond and printed and bound in Canada.
Printed on 100% post-consumer recycled paper.

First Printing: 2010

The publisher gratefully acknowledges the financial support of the Canada Council for the Arts; the Government of Canada through the Book Publishing Industry Development Program; and the Province of British Columbia through the British Columbia Arts Council and the Book Publishing Tax Credit for our publishing activities.

Library and Archives Canada Cataloguing in Publication

Morse, Garry Thomas
After Jack / Garry Thomas Morse.

Poems.
ISBN 978-0-88922-630-2

I. Title.

PS8626.O774A65 2010 C811'.6 C2009-906975-X

Contents

After Jack

with an Introduction
by Jack Spicer

Introduction

Sadly, this manuscript which once felt so fresh & funny to me has become part of a sickly tradition of whispers That is not to say popular tunes exactly, but since some young stragglers are hanging around this madman as if they were listening I will be careful about everything I don't say

Plagiarism aside, these poems are not translations I am sympathetic since it is clear that Mr. Morse was handed some pallid assignment, such as to dump a glacier on my body of work & then break the ice, extracting some dead school of letters like the skeleton of a prehistoric fish I will allow Mr. Morse some leeway in his oily escapism, since he is stumbling from pub to pub so tenaciously & slamming tables so ludicrously & shouting into stranger faces so passionately that he is working in the medium of Jack Spicer

That remains open to speculation In some cases, he has entirely ignored my own translations & has found a more understanding friend in Mr. Lorca In other cases, he has taken advantage of my translations & adapted them to his own politic or personal matters, even peppered with Yiddish slang, which is incomprehensible dreck to one of the deceased In addition, there are some poems which have no point of reference, no origin whatsoever Sandwiching between Mr. Lorca & myself, Mr. Morse brings up something of a three-headed dog's breakfast in bed

However, in spite of my complaints, I feel a touch of warmth (always a comfort to the dead) with regard to Mr. Morse Not as many as you might think come knocking & few so young & full of blood & ready to slip into a bathing suit of the imagination How awkward for the dead to admit they are smitten, even when they are so obviously past it Well, these days we seem to have drugs for everything

I knew, of course, it was just a matter of time before some young thing would come along & believe in magic again Even in the margins between life & idealized language, there is still room for something to live, for notes to exist & tones to brood until they can make their break into the world Like a compromised starlet on a cinematic witness stand, I swear before you & the jury out there that Mr. Morse had his wicked way with me & in the same breath I *was* rather provocatively jacketed

The letters are not a problem I realize that Mr. Morse suffers from episodes of loneliness & still acknowledges their importance I realize he has let a promising career languish in lieu of chasing me down the dusty aisles of libraries & secondhand booksellers Even if his eye is roving from the page & he is writing me in the vain hope of amplifying his broadcast for some lady in the distance, I wish him the best of luck in that affair & honey, I hope he's worth it

In fact, Mr. Morse comes off as so serious about what he calls his Art, I refuse to crack a single joke at his expense I have thought of a wise reader & friend who says heaven is a British pub I refuse to spoil that surprise, as well

Jack Spicer
Waiting in the trunk with Orpheus, 2010

Clarence Malcolm Lowry

translation for Paul

Ecstasy in the white
pages of nards, salt
& spunk unlimited

White, the sheet
is moulting black
bird feathers

Red eyes burnt out
surfing some dream
Outside, the shakes

In the white pages
what a big wet hole
in this ecstasy

In the white pages
Nards Salt Spunk

The Dirty Sleepwalker

translation for a Muse in transition

Brown, I want you brown
so brown out of my life

Your brown corduroy coat, can
I take it back to Sally Ann

O eyes in roadside mud rifts
I finger your whole body in

bowling shoes Brown with
constipated words & brown

runs upon porcelain pages
brown the round you never

bought O fuck that farkuckt
colour of chinos & Forever

lipstick Brown the weather
tomorrow & brown the terrier

leaving soft tentative turds
& brown stenches of your *yes*

Brown, I want you brown
so brown out of my life

Monotones

translation for Tara v9.1

You were lipred when the sun
rose & I was obsidian

You were weedgreen when the dawn
broke & I was obsidian

You were ashblond when noon
struck & I was obsidian

You were lipred when the sun
set & I was obsidian

You were raven when the lights
went out & I was obsidian

You were plumblue when the moon
fell & I was obsidian

You were lipred when the sun
rose & I was obsidian

Bring Me the Luminous One

translation for s/h

Bring me La Niña de los Peines
Bring me that girl of the combs

Hot as fire-water brandy
I find her hair in my food

I do not think s/he will dance for me
I do not think s/he can sing to me

Bring me El Niño de los Peines
Bring me that boy of the combs

With scarlet plumage like a fire-
ant peacock, freshly blowtorched

s/he flamencos with defiant feet
& deconstructs on 80s night

O bring me the damage
in manzanilla & cazalla

& bring me one more shot
of Niña, girl of the combs

Dear Jack,

I write belatedly but you are well aware late is better than never Another beauty around the corner & some thing awakens A black dog sits on the red hexagons with paws beseechingly stretched out He looks up at the new beauty with longing eyes Poems are like this, like dogs in the way since you need nothing else Just a quick lick once in a while All these other lives appear garish in contrast with that black dog, including mine Ah, the pleasure of recording another beauty & this black dog At any moment I could fall to the floor of red hexagons in love, only the dog The dog has more fidelity in that look We return to each other in good faith

Beautiful women & beautiful pints would fade to black without this meditating dog who keeps me honest, who rises to plead with opal eyes for my bowl of chicken soup Hunger is not desire Thirst is not thirst I'm sure you know that if I know you at all What a lot neither of us knows The dog lies on his side, eyeing the red hexagons as if begging to be understood A sharp whistle & a familiar hand of affection ruffles his black fur Is that what I expect after all or am I just talking to myself or barking to a moon that is only the sound of a dropped dish

These slurred odes to solitude are nothing to a pair of wits in the corner But will they blurt out a relic of talk I'll let you know someday That would be news to me Meanwhile, the dog's eyes ask me to be faithful to the rain, the beauty, my touch of fever, etc He comes over to lick crumbs from my fingers You don't like dogs, the beauty states I have no time to answer since I'm chatting with you, Jack There is never not a danger of being utterly misunderstood Pleasure in concentration, in perception, might look outward, unsmiling The rain, the beauty, the fever, the dog who smiles with his tail Even these shadows of reality on the page are unable to betray my poker face How to translate

It seems a waste to feel you up at some afterlife party & then give you a lecture the next morning Feeling goes on behind the words Were the naked words enough for you Were five senses enough for you I don't know how you can write with all this noise, the beauty asks She will go on asking because she can't hear you or me exactly She will ask again & I will crawl to the next watering hole How can I write without it, Jack Could you

Love,
Garry

Ballad of the 11 Passages

translation for Glen

Spelling Jack_Spicer
implicates 11 letters

Spell with the white
space in your heart

Rimbaud was always older
Are we live, Jack_Spicer

Spell with the white
space in your heart

Beauty He was right on top
of it Why not write it off

There was a token black
vowel, his mother's gums

At this hour it is sad
& hard to spell any thing

Damn you damn you 1 night
I will find all 11 letters

Remember when the alphabet was
a breathy almanac for ploughing

Remember when the alphabet was
dirty pictures of animals

The rest of us are still
coming down in that barn

& Jack_Spicer, I would
love to say rent/free

Spell with the white
space in your heart

Marcel Duchamp

translation for Emily & Thor

Hip hop, I've given you
all & now I'm nothing

Kanye's for cunts, she
said, drunk & swinging

Sometimes you gotta stop
& smell the hellflowers

I have issues relating
to CGI creature voices

Hip hop, I've given you
all & now I'm nothing

Your phone is already
our next museum item

Your phone is already
everything but phone

This is just like the 2nd
to last episode of The O.C.

Hip hop, I've given you
all & now I'm nothing

I fantasize about *Friends*
being on *Without a Trace*

then that snap of me & Echo
You will never find that snap

then that snap of my wedding
You will never find that snap

Hip hop, I've given you
all & now I'm nothing

Elementary Memetics

translation for Aubyn

If a train is going X kilos
how much will a gram cost

If the sun is blocked out
how much closer is Heraclitus

If a budget is balanced
what is poetry's gross

Marketa has curves
She dances outside

If a tour bus is going Y
how much to ride under it

If Diderot can disprove God
can algebra prove Taylor Swift

If Q shipments of waste
what is the rate of algae

Marketa has curves
She dances outside

If a body is lying in the sun
how many hours until forgotten

If Wagner had hugged him more
what could Nietzsche teach you

If *if* translates into yew tree
how many ifs form a rich forest

Marketa has curves
She dances outside

The Echognomic Crisis

translation for a

Pretty as a preening robot owl
we could never hear over engine

missing the jamb of words
missing the point entirely

of howling into the flowing
river of vowels, of stalking

pebbly trail along knowing
of your name, of wolving &

owling the most preening
& prowling of creatures

pretty as a gleaming gleaning vowel
we could never hear over language

nor awkward flush of backward love
reinforced with Coriolis Force

missing the lamb of wolves
missing the oink entirely

like lining up loves in a row
like laughter off a love's back

mewling into loopy bewilderness
you could never love a semantic

nor pan opera from Outaouais
nor tan the hide of a speak

nor suffer a casual duck
nor be considered moose

pretty as a screaming robot O
we could never hear over whelp

Trocadero

translation for Padam

The bastards! Clowns with
brobdingnagian cocks in 1

utility vehicle they've taken
all our chicks (some of them

boys) The bastards! They
put snails in our lettuce

lettuce in our gastropods
& Tito Gobbi's codpiece

thrown into grocery boy
carts, what is that to

do with the $$$$$ of eggs
I can't work under these

conditionings The bastards!
They're taking all our jobs

turning all our tricks
& picking all our locks

unspeakable skeletons in
every closet The bastards!

Wagner

translation for Ahmed

Soundless, my shadow
moves through the dikes

Then my shadow is ack-
nowledged master of stars

Shadow, you send my
flesh calm reflections

Huge, my shadow moves
like a violet knish

A hundred crickets
want gold to go up

Light spawns inside me
reflected in the dikes

Metamorph

translation for Jack

Tonight there is
no plash to talk of

A digital frog
may PLOP

on your erect head
no Basho you imagine

more of the old queer
bashing in the park

or industrial waste
stilting the stream

of information, yet
don't adjust your set

on the friggin' blink
before you even blink

some one is croaking for
help across the rain of

centuries, spotted frogs
trapped as fat tadpoles

& tonight there is
no plash to talk of

That Punctured Inflatable Love

translation for Ken

SPINNING COCK: O the futility!

(*Pan to a black bell shape in a meadow outside a rustridden farmhouse, hunched over a rickety bamboo cane*)

CHARLIE CHAPLIN (*lifts cane like a ukulele & gently strums a serenade of velvetythroated silence*):

O come to the pane
The fields are ripe
with freshly laid
cow dung dollops

O come to the pane
& peel your eyes
taters are being
beaten aubergine

O come to the pane
& peel your ears
green corn can hear
green pods opening

O starladen udders
O lactescent hormones
Cows are the universe
turned inside/out

O come to the pane
The fields are ripe
with cow dung & I
am knee deep in it

DEBUTANTE OF THE YEAR (*purses lips in a large O & wraps a box of tampons in a spotted hankie & ties them to Charlie's very flexible stick, which he has tossed aloft*): I am coming out

SPINNING COCK (*ironically*): Hey, some cocks are trying to sleep here & ain't she a little young to cock-a-doodle-diddle-doo

DEBUTANTE OF THE YEAR (*busts her father's condom machine & knots together those sturdy prophylactic corn protectors into a makeshift rope of Rough Riders*): Eep

CHARLIE CHAPLIN: Don't cream your drawers, my love, I is a-coming

(*There is a comical scene where Chuck tries to climb the slippery rope like an Indian fakir & keeps landing on his duff with split seams*)

DEBUTANTE OF THE YEAR: I'm coming out Catch me daddy-o

CHARLIE CHAPLIN (*sidesplittingly lascivious*): Come to daddy

(*The Debutante of the Year smiles quizzically, sidles the circuit of goo-ey condoms & slides down them like a firefighter's pole She lands on Charlie's head & deep beneath her dress with Venus Man-trap patterns his little black bowler begins to dance*)

DEBUTANTE OF THE YEAR: That feels swell, mister Pleased to make your acquaintance

(*The Debutante of the Year cocks her head to one side underneath her hat & the stage lights reveal it is in fact Clara Bow Charlie shakes her hand vigorously from underneath her dress*)

CLARA BOW (*winking to offscreen lover*): Them boys call me Clara

FARMER DEXTROSE (*waving hoe*): Get that tramp outta yer flowerbed

(*Charlie emerges with a gelatinous substance on his little moustache & moves his eyes from side to side angelically, shrugging emphatically like Pierre Trudeau*)

FARMER DEXTROSE (*shaking rake & going all* American Gothic *on the couple*): Get rid of that flat-ass broke sonofabitch!

(*There is an uproarious scene where the farmer tries to rake & hoe his daughter home & Charlie foils every attempt, hooking the old boy backward with the bamboo stick of Stayfree*)

SPINNING COCK: If I were you, little tramp, I'd KrazyGlue myself to this chick I hear her uncle owns Ticketmaster & Expedia & Hotels.com No more sleeping in Needle Park USA

CHARLIE CHAPLIN (*tipping his hat gallantly & tossing a limp Clara over his right shoulder*): I hit paydirt

CLARA BOW: Which way to Albuquerque

(*The Cock spins wildly on the roof & points up the road Butterflies emerge from the farmer's furious beard & begin to bite into his unprotected stalks of genetically modified corn They drop dead in such a holocaust that the farmer is caught off guard & Charlie & his third wife have time to toddle off*)

CHARLIE CHAPLIN (*kicking gargantuan front yard crucifix to the ground between him & Farmer Dextrose*): So long you big fascist

CLARA BOW (*before talkies*): Is this tramp really a millionaire in disguise

(*Pan to bowels of the Vatican Bank A priest is stuffing thick denominations in the folds of his robes A young male waif on his lap watches, agape Charlie struts in, perfectly bowlegged, stashing his statutory charge behind a weeping pietà*)

CHARLIE CHAPLIN: I want to make an honest woman of this one, etc

MONSIGNORE BENEDICK (*petting boy gravely*): What are your thoughts re: the Big Guy upstairs

(*Charlie gesticulates without hubris but with hamartia, acknowledging there is some power higher than his hat, etc He adds a wanking motion for effect, followed by a finger wagging tsk tsk & a slapping of his wrist*)

MONSIGNORE BENEDICK: Your conviction is noted

(*Charlie glowers murderously & makes like he is going to hit the road but Clara Bow stares into his soul & gives him a transubstantial wink as if to say yes, but that won't improve my situation, will it Chuck*)

MONSIGNORE BENEDICK: All of the Lord's children deserve a second chance Charlie, my child, all manner of holiness is invested in this here pennyfarthing With this, you can distribute the Word from villa to villa & perhaps one day you will find redemption for your incessant horndogging & insatiable promiscuity & conveniently lascivious pratfalls & randy pelvic dances & soggy crimes of the imagination in hellfire & brimstone

(*Charlie nods shamefacedly & twitches from both the rebuke & last night's bender He tosses the priest's literature into a rosecoloured basket & hops on the pennyfarthing with grace He mimes pedalling against the wind as CNN cues the Mother Teresa: Road to Sainthood music*)

LT SBIRRO (*cameo by Harvey Keitel, firing shots into the air*): Hey fruitcake Get off the fucking bike

OFFICER MALEFATTA (*cameo by Joe Pesci*): Now I gotta fill out a fucking report on some fucking fruit fuck on jesus christ a fucking funny bike

LT SBIRRO (*fondling pistol & rubbing nostrils impatiently*): Alright let's go, funny boy

OFFICER MALEFATTA (*knocking Charlie off his pennyfarthing with a truncheon & breaking his flexible stick in two over one knee*): You think this fucking physical humour shit is funny I'll give you physical humour shit, you fat fucking beggar fuck You think I'm funny, huh

(*Charlie dusts off his tails & smiles adorably & shrugs emphatically to communicate his ignorance of the legal system*)

LT SBIRRO (*sniffing sardonically at the thought of playing good cop*): You better answer He ain't having such a good day

OFFICER MALEFATTA (*beating Charlie half unconscious with Billy Whip*): This fuck don't talk much this fucking piece of fucking shit

CHARLIE CHAPLIN (*widening arms & spitting blood*): It went like this My hat fell over my eyes & I ended up wrapping fish in these holy holy pamphlets & you can see the Lord's fingerprints on the fins

LT SBIRRO (*leaning pinkcandyflosscoloured pennyfarthing against a very old & celebrated wall*): These don't look like no psalms to me More like poems or filthy fucking limericks & what have we here Take a fucking look at that, Joe

OFFICER MALEFATTA (*eyeing centrefold of young boy in blue thong*): You sick fuck you fucking sick fuck No *Sports Illustrated* Swimsuit Issue for you, huh You're the twisted cocksucking fuck we been lookin' for

(*Charlie stares down at his pant leg & shoe, under which a small puddle is forming*)

LT SBIRRO (*slipping white packets deftly into his overcoat*): Some buttmonkey's been downloading minors on the Internet

(*The consigliere arrives He kicks the pennyfarthing with his pointed loafer & it deflates Then he rips up the rose basket in a display of strength & throws the pennyfarthing on a freshly lit bonfire There is much patting of bottoms & swearing & champagne poured all around They begin to fill Charlie's empty pockets with bricks & stones & mime a man being hung from a bridge Everyone titters at that*)

CHARLIE CHAPLIN (*gathering up the ashes of poems & songs & dabbing his eyes & blowing his schnozz with a filthy hankie*): Ma biciclettà

(*Clara Bow enters arm-in-arm with Monsignore Benedick, sporting a huge belly & with her hands alone informs Charlie of a visitation during the night Her eyes are limpid & brimming over with The Absolute Truth Charlie pulls out a watch fob & points at it as if to say excellent timing my love, really great, yeah*)

MONSIGNORE BENEDICK (*pointing to Clara's effulgent belly*): I have administered all my guidance & protection to this child & she is plum up the duff

OFFICER MALEFATTA: If she's got pardon my French one in the fucking oven, then who's the cuntfucking baker

MONSIGNORE BENEDICK (*pointing to Charlie*): Thou art the man

(*Monsignore Benedick has a word with the consigliere They pinch toches playfully & then Benedick places a package on the dash of his limousine The consigliere gives a final motion & then speeds away*)

OFFICER MALEFATTA: Don't fucking tell me we gotta let this fucking looney toon bumfucking bum off the fucking hook

LT SBIRRO: (*handing back broken walking stick to Charlie*) He's not our patsy Honest mistake No hard feelings You're free to go, to church anyway

OFFICER MALEFATTA (*eyeing Clara Bow, who is winking at him*): Fucking talk about out of the frying pan & into the shotgun weddin'

(*The officers escort Charlie up to the altar at gunpoint His pants fall down repeatedly, much to the amusement of the officers as he fans himself with his hat & rubs his concussion, looking up the winding road nervously toward looming spires It is getting dark*)

CHARLIE CHAPLIN: Oy gevalt

(*Charlie waddles up & down the aisle as the bridal chorus begins to play His eyes dart to & fro but all the exits are bolted with giant economysize crosses*)

LT SBIRRO (*with shotgun to the little tramp's back*): Quit stalling

OFFICER MALEFATTA: Yeah, this should be the happiest day of your life you fucking fuckedup fuck

MONSIGNORE BENEDICK: We are gathered together today …

FARMER DEXTROSE (*shaking hands with Charlie*): Sorry about the misunderstanding Now I understand this is all legit I want you all to know that she has a wealthy uncle who owns GlobalPorn.cum & everything will be just fine & dandy for the piccolo bambino

(*Charlie nods very very enthusiastically & French kisses his new father-in-law in profound adulation*)

CHARLIE CHAPLIN: I have seen the Light

SPINNING COCK: You'll be back, you goddamned hypocrite

(*Clara bow winks & the curtains close around her protruding belly*)

CLARA BOW'S BELLY: Ka ching ka ching

Ballad of the Promiscuous Birds

translation for Warren

¡The birds are
not monogamous!

Their feathers
are taken off

The sun in my eyes
The moon in my ears

No longer passive
O passive no more

Don't look any longer
Don't listen any more

¡The verbs are
not monogamous!

They're taking off
voices of leather

The sun in my eyes
The moon in my ears

No longer active
O active no more

¡The words are
not monogamous!

Their red plumes
are taken off

& one was the other
& both were neither

Suicide Wings

translation for Danny

It was 5 in the twilight
A face was breaking in

pave/ment But his soul
      bailed out & sat on the ledge

O dissipated angel in a
lonely room There is no

lonely with Hank Williams
his soul insisted over a

broken face below, grey
the cassette player in his

soul's rheumatic hands as a dog-
eared snap of his dead brother

Next time I take the stairs
I wanted to laugh but didn't

He handed me the ruined tape
as a thieving crowd thronged

A Mickey Mouse watch stopped
It was 5 in the twilight

Bacchus

translation for Laura

Deep in the horrible forest
a young lady carves oranges

Peels each sliver
of an orange moon

The moon talks with dogs
Mistaken, she starts over

Elsewhere, the lady finds bay
leaves in her bowl of gazpacho

Bay leaves adorn
corners of night

In such corners, neither my life
nor my heart will shoo silverfish

Huntress in a cold bowl
she carries a cold knife

Peels her blood orange
dress in private dance

Tonight, she hunts for hidden
membranes—terrible & extended

The Little Halfwit

translation for Tara v8.7

I phoned you after
noon & it was sticky

People were peering
through the glass

Did they see any
thing you didn't say

I phoned you again
A bad connection …

Would she show up
What would develop

I phoned you again
I didn't even talk

That tone was final
I ran out of silver

A finger in the slot
& nothing was there

I phoned you after
noon & it was sticky

Scented Candle in the Wind of My Vacuum 1891

translation for Arthur & Donato

Salut, my colloquial little slut
Although you didn't even take off
Like a proper upstanding Parnassian
A mere caesura away from thirty-six

Acing every exercise and *examen*
Cramming each up a fresh behind
To really see what a seer could see
Down the vomitous gutter of time

By the time the wick of your erudition
Reached the flaming bowels of genius
You had already taken off, giving up
Writing for gun running, suspected

Dead. Good riddance! Needing
Your love like a hole in the hand
Washed down with warm glass
Of sulfuric acid is not healthy

You pissed all over our Venus
Leaving her verminous green
With your big little instrument
The colour of crapulous toads

In imaginary sewage. The city
Was invented by an architect
Who sang the key to it, losing
It through a hole in your pants

Vindictive steampunk, you
Ruined their crisp new suits
With bubbly visionary spit
With unspeakable stains

Art, go vowel your hell off!
Mindfuck somebody else!
Your candle is a gargantuan
Stub—and it doesn't count!

Verlaine

translation for Guy

In needle park tonight, I
want to unbutton my verse

Mercy on my soul
I didn't mean it

Straddle that soft caesura
& meet me in the wormwood

Mercy on my soul
I didn't mean it

Tonight I beat my wife
& beat off Art to boot

Mercy on my soul
I didn't mean it

Tonight there's baby tossing
& bumfucking Art to boot

Mercy on my soul
I didn't mean it

Another phosphorous, *merde*!
& I'll stop I swear

Mercy on my soul
I didn't mean it

I am a superb poet
A pathetic fallacy

Mercy on my soul
I didn't mean it

Dear Jack,

Translation: little movers with big hearts Forgive a dead metaphor from the side of a passing truck

Translation: a foreign flight where luggage is easily lost But was it really so satisfying or uplifting to find your duffel bag was not lifted or your skis were not broken or your attaché case made it through with your person As we speak they are examining the pseudonyms of others & probing their bodies with long beeping sticks

If unlucky for you it comes to a search of your person there might be nothing to discover but a small stash in your drawers To be safe I swallow mine Comes out the next morning like nobody's business What objects are they looking for & what are we trying to hide Jingling coins or jangling keys or misplaced & suspiciously bent utensils What objects survive that horrible beeping Is that translation, Jack

Then what is worse, a covert agent or a terrorist poem slipping through borders of the mind How about a hefty tourist in a shirt from Maui, shaking his moneymaker for all it's worth, beeping madly & throwing all manner of paraphernalia out of his laden pockets Not only a spectacle but a *live* exhibit for local or global media Language is a little too subtle, malleable, palpable, savoury, buttery & shaggy for that Language may be in a disguise, with or without a beard Also to catch a phrase in the teeth is kind of deadly Time to call for a little vocab

Somebody hammered somebody's head into the ground in the good book I mean that is how some handle words meaning nothing It is the graph of a head splitting open Those types get pretty zealous & zanied all the same waving around them dead words on pikes like freshly sharpened pencils But words are stuck under restaurant tables too They stick to your feet & get caught in your hair You sure you wanna use a pike for that now

Translation: pencils break Tongues are bitten Gum pops & gets stale & flaccid Whether we were chatting in Mandarin or Martian or Martial I understood your lewd gestures all the same, Jack What recollects value is a certain stick-to-it-ness Right now I am clinging to something I am beating it off because it is so long & cold & hard Also, it is beeping

Is that you, Jack

Love,
Garry

Song of Logging the Earth

translation for Jaclyn

Silviculturist
Hack down my shadow
Free me from this pain
of waking without limbs

¿Mirrors on the ceiling?
Morning revolves around
me & night photocopies
me in each of her stars

I want to live without
images, without a self
dreaming pandas & owls
are my leaves & birds

Silviculturist
Hack down my shadow
Free me from this pain
of waking without limbs

Casida for Those Who K'vetch

translation for You Know Who You Are

Beyond the brand new white
wall, there is blubbering

Weeping on brand new trucks
Weeping on shiny new nipples

Beyond the brand new white
wall, there is blubbering

Some thing in the eyes of Robsonstrasse
Some thing in the eyes of Robson.com

Beyond the brand new white
wall, there is blubbering

Tears on her whale cosmetics
Tears on his mail-order cock

Beyond the brand new white
wall, there is blubbering

All over a cable cut
All over a phone un-
hooked

Narcissus

translation for Garry

Dear sir, so saturate, so
full of gall, did you fall in

that drink Down there it is
dirty I like the drink dirty

you dirty boy, to watch the
cocks fight ¡Watch them fight!

My eyes stumbled &
fell into that swill

Your hair felt thick
& coarse down there

¡O yeah, baby!
¿Was that it? ¡Pretty boy!

… another round of the same

Lost in that drink, I
remembered No I don't

¡Es Verdad!

translation for Kathryn

¡What labo***u***r it is to
love you as I love you!

Because of your love
there is pain in the air
there is pain in the head
there is pain in the heart
there is pain in the pants

¿Who will buy this pair
of stain-resistant slacks
with pockets full of tears
& who will carry such a
burden of love to tear
them apart in the dark?

¡What labor it is to
love you as I love you!

Anode for Walt Whitman

translation for Mariner

Deep in the East River, boys
are singing in concrete briefs
doused in dark oil & glowing
in a salad spinner millions
of feet are Eschering up
& down the Mall of America
to shlep home for a whirl

But no one sleeps (gay schluffen)
& no one drinks the walnutgrey water
& no one loves the blue veins in leaves
& no one loves the beach draped in oil
& no one listens to poetry

Deep in the East River
cinematic boys are asking
in b/w about waste in the
oil, being waste in the
river & no one buys oil
Paul Newman is hawking

But no one stops
no one tires of exhaust
no one hears a single help me
nor buds & weeds buds & weeds
nor an old queen asking ¿hash, dear?
nor our heroine in the junk-sick dawn

& when the moon rises
osteoporosis will arrive
over needles in the grass
& memory will soon be
dragged away by white
coats & why can't we film
those coffins coming home
a reporter asks on CNN
I mean out of respect

O city of optic death & wires
O city of no fun stuck in the mud
¿What angel dust deep inside your cement?

¿What self-service ethanol deep inside your cars?
¿What terrible dream of dead anemones?

Not once, Walt Whitman, sweet old shtupper
have I failed to see your beard full of butterflies
exquisitely perched upon ears & ears
of genetically altered corn They
scream like horny birds given
discount vasectomies but
it is perfectly safe says a man
in an airless suit I repeat he says
it is perfectly safe to have
a beard full of butterflies
& to have your tubes tied

Not once, proliferous prick
have a laser-blasted pair of
eyes peered through the smog
to catch you relaxed on Xanax
to find you fishing for rubbers
to go to bed with your Vicodin
to get it up for your Viagra

Not once, Braggadocio, Long
Dong Machismo, Mail-Order Cock
lovely old lech, Walt Whitman
have I seen you in licensed bars
or pinching over-age grocery
boys or dragging a basket
full of mysteries up
& down the fluorescent
aisles of Davie Village

Not once in Capers were you
hunting for virile vitamins
in that paradise of collards
& swiss chard & happy chickens
also tired of eating happy chicken

¡También ése! ¡Him too! & they
sit on your damp face & wrap your
body of work in yesterday's sopping
headlines & something is fishy:
Jim & Tim or Rob & Bob or Ken &
Ben are going to tie the knot
(their tubes are neatly tied)
After that, everyone else will be
well hung in a locker of dead meat

Not once in our global
Safeway did a Czech kid
upc your binary can of
consommé & finger your
wad of glossy coupons
& fondle your id card
& scan your sweet name
& on impulse winking
whisper Walt Whitman
who is driving these
groceries home tonight
& no I do not need help
no thank you not even
from you Walt Whitman

¡También ése! ¡Him too! Dirty
digits pilfering your Gucci bag
of dreams, polegreasers & back
slappers, our forbidden apples
ridden with wormmail & reamed
up to here with invisible spam
while boys & their semi-automatic
organs are sold under bridges of
code

¿When will the redskins show up
in the blue wardrobe of cavalry
with attaché cases to go along
& fresh spit on their moccasins
& not everyone had wigwams
not even teepees Walt Whitman
not even this hybrid Indian
luftmensch

well, we used to be Indians
now we're all First Nations
& that means the last to
know in a dead language?

Yet browsing through search engines & *I
Saw You* columns for the perfect pale nude
salty as a sea rose in oblivious waters
I found they had fucked with the map
of you, Walt Whitman, with your
body & the mesh of your face

Now the morning after, they won't
even sell me the remedy at Walmart
not among the self-serve self-help
nor among islands of cash registers
where they are hunting customers
with elephantitantic pricing guns
& who the hell sold me this strap-on
that glimmers in the slipshod dawn

I will take it back tomorrow but
don't even talk to me of dreams
they seem to have shanghaied you
Walt Whitman, on some ship bound
for bottles with no return, lost
in that drink of locally brewed
rats & avaricious seagulls Just
don't even talk to me of dreams

Settle down, settle down
with some soft barnacle
settle down, settle down
with some shiny cubic
zirconia since fake
diamonds are forever

Nah, I won't say nada, old fart, Walt
Whitman, against some boy who embroiders
the name Martha™ neatly into his pillow
nor against two studs who want
to tie the knot on television
nor former Vegas performers
selling Pilates & Personal
Power, not even those who love
to look & are not in the market
just browsing
                    But you insipid cybernetic
knobfiddling browntongued cityboysluts
slithering up corporate ladders
like flaccid adders
                          you utter toches-leckers
                          you sell the flesh
of others
            even you, our local Caesar
            you're giving it to me nicely
            burning at both ends with no
            grease, just dripping wax
            promises & why can't I get
            sloshed too

Ever & ever against you & those
who sell their liberty on eBay
& poison our soil & sell us more
seeds & kick us out of our homes
& tamper with the drugs they sell
us & sell sell sell until there
are drugs in the food, forever
against you patent cannibal
supremacists of the US
thread cutters in Mexico
poppy wearers in Pakistan
uzi hawkers in British mosques
tv digitalis panderers in Germany
bear bladder peddlers in China
young diseased pimps in Manila
olive oil apothecaries in Italy
seed pushers in starving Africa
inaudible complainers in Canada

Sleepwalkers of the whole world
wholesale online factories of
flesh & devourers of dungholes
pornography is downloading you

[30 seconds remaining …]

¡No quarter for you! Death
drips from the industrial complex
in your eyes & you are better dressed
in the fetid alley of dead flowers
¡No quarter! I have my own habit
to look after Let the baffled
the pure, the neoclassical cocks
clean enough to eat off of turn
like large skeletons in the lock
& slam the whole city in your face

& you, ravishing white Walt Whitman
I see you asleep outside *The Hudson*
(they are building more leaky condos)
as your beard & snot become

beautiful icicles & frozen
your hands are open & you
are muttering if you lick the pole
it will stick if you lick the pole
it will stick & no one sees
the SUV strike you to the
curb, a shadow of the last
some extinct snow leopard

Sleep then sleep Nothing to see here
Only the Interior is burning & only
the world is flooded with machines
& tears Reheat the pubescent wind
of leftover night & wake up Wake
up & look at the lame hybrid lad
marching along & whacking off
his melting pot in the cold
his cross-fertilized friend
convulsing in a gutter
of empty tinsel towns &
unsound surround-sound
& no one yells fire

& the wheat starts to
awaken & the potatoes
pry open their eyes
& the fields turn
to flaming heads
full of gasoline

& no one yells fire
& no one yells fire

Central Park

translation for Vicky

It happens
at the zoo

Some bears
stood me up

Some dad washed
his hands of goats

We had a short row
& there was a storm

You bought some home-
less dude a hamburger

He said I'm good
How about a soda

I bought a T-shirt
to show where I was

Even the monkeys
had a good shriek

& all that muggy afternoon, we
were never mugged in the green

It happens
at the zoo

Phew, That Was Close

translation for Robin

The angels have landed
like bloated seagulls

upon crooked railings
upon leaky roofs
&
the faux owl has
fallen
        stricken by wind

The angels have landed
like bloated seagulls

They wail beige psalms
for winded sycophants

& blow the ivory tusks
of reprobate elephants

The angels have landed
like bloated seagulls

Purple starfish stick
in their soft gullets

& they bully crows
for a bit of bread

The angels have landed
like bloated seagulls

upon crooked railings
upon leaky roofs

have left their blessing
upon our foggy windshield

¡Ssshhhhh!

translation for Tony

I don’t want to
I don’t want to
tell you fuck all

Deep in your eyes
2 limbs have withered

with sap
with breeze
with laughter
with gold

They were shaking

I don’t want to
I don’t want to
tell you fuck all

Frustration

translation for Debbie

Candle, match
& gasoline

A moth beats
wings against glass

Candle, match
& gasoline

A woman surpasses
posteriority

Candle, match
& gasoline

A cackle
breaks the dark

Candle, match
& gasoline

A wasp reads
its last paper

Candle, match
& gasoline

A man asks
quietly for water

Dear Jack,

Red hair like bottled henna about a set of wily crooked teeth Were the teeth or their red-haired owner wily She may not be crooked or bright as her red treatment As you see with your fleshy mouth & absent eyes words are a gamble & the house of language rules I may observe she has red hair, she is shapely but wily, crooked or bright is unknown & that is poetry

Provocative as a freeway billboard, her image asks to be taken with me She is a static manifestation of despair, or so I imagine, some DNA chimaera of need & desire, pure thought tossed onto the passenger side of a speeding vehicle like a smutty foreign magazine or glossy catalogue My mind flips through at leisure, that leg, that smaller breast, that hint of skin, that outfit, that new *do* Obsession with the *real* has nothing on her neck & wrists & smile & silence & frown & pain & face flushed with rage when he asks her to get in the fucking truck right now

Her perfume is a synthetic process, bottled & sold & rubbercemented to the posterior of some pixelated celebrity with a translucent face They are edited & fart roses while we carry on with our stale bread & geranium breath Only the poem is singular to that perfume, that overwhelming cloud which loiters in elevators for a very long time When were you first slapped on This morning How sweet or now I am sneezing People are starting to stare At a smell So the imagination aches to concatenate itself to that whiff of mystery, that promise of the physical & there is talk in this lift

This perfume of idle babillage is not Baudelaire's musty flask or smell-o-vision or the scented cloud of passing women in Montréal who so compelled my great-grandfather Levy to chase & perhaps proposition them with takings from the rag trade All my relations are this perfume, since objects are the establishment of relations or correspondences Are you still chasing her, great-grandfather Levy, or did you catch her by now I smell this gestalt beauty & my blood is up Is this genetically modified memory or merely objects talking in a quiet corner of the elevator which drones to life, going down The doors will shudder open with a mechanical sigh of relief & I will see a phantasmagoria of perfume-wearers & smell their breath from lunch & touch your face like alien braillings in the lift & wonder is it really you Jack & who is that with you, Federico

This is instead the scent of a malamute kicking up the earth with its hind legs so another dog may scent the same patch of ground or base of streetlamp & get the message & partake in honest democracy Perhaps I should be angry that I have been roped into this fakir rope trick & into a single link of this cold eternal chain letter If you find this, young poet, you will know what to do You have mail

Love,
Garry

Ballad of Booze & Good Books

translation for Blair

My bowels are on fire
like people in the Bible

Language is jammed
in such congestion

Words come out like
food caught in phlegm

My bowels are on fire
like people in the Bible

The moon a sallow bitch
who hounds sleepy dogs

The sun a floor wax shine
to pissholes in the snow

My bowels are on fire
like people in the Bible

I fear a millipede
fallen in my mane

I fear this head ache's
tent peg thru my head

My bowels are on fire
like people in the Bible

Ballad of Stalking Presences

translation for Colette

I want the water to get lost
I want the wind to get lost

I want an evening without eyes
I want my heart plucked of gilt

I want bullshit to advise large leaves
I want a blind double-sexed death of gloom

I want skull teeth to shine
I want yellows to soak silk

I see the sword of wounded night
& her violent embrace with noon

I beat off a sunset of sangria
killing time in the golden arches

But don't turn on the light
black cactus behind the blind

Leave me the madness of dark planets
Stop flashing your blatant waist

Ballad of Entropic Despair

translation for Kim

They are breaking
my coat is breaking

(When I awoke my pockets
were full of books)

They are leaking
my shoes are leaking

(When I awoke my soles
were full of water)

It is cutting
my wrists, cutting

(When I awoke my arms
were full of paper)

It is cutting
me, cutting me

(When I awoke my eyes
were full of your self)

Ballad of Amargo, the Bitter One

translation for Soma

The water smiles nearby
Teeth of foam, lips of ice

¿What are you selling
girl, so nicely stacked?

Sir, I sell
alcohol

¿What are you carrying
mixed with your blood?

Sir, I carry
alcohol

¿Your tears of tequila
where are they from?

Sir, I weep
alcohol

¿Your bitterness
where is it from?

Do you want to
try the bitter

Dear Jack,

How drunk were you when you heard those poems being written How about lending me a few loonies (with inflation) for a similar cause Leave a promissory note in my left shoe, the one with frayed laces Right now I feel tipsy enough to drink in the looks of beauty & take her by surprise What time do you get off Hell I feel fucking sexy Muy caliente & you better believe it

Looks good on paper, anyway I am concerned about such adolescent poems that so readily prostitute themselves in order to get an eyeful of the world There they are again, sticking an alluring foot out on the information superhighway & well don't you worry they might get picked up Just look at their deconstructed clothing It's old hat I know but sometimes I think you don't love their form at all You just love their fishy guts Ha ha, but the poems that pluck out their false eyelashes later & vigorously rub off their layers of make-up over many hours or even centuries They have a hidden promise This may be suggestive but you start to think of pulling out their gold teeth while they are sleeping

It is unfortunate how friends & lovers become props for the poet, especially in those moments the bubble bursts & words spill out of a mouth in no particular order & they apply a damp cloth to those dirty lips & then the poet calls his or her page & returns to do battle within the canvas, with nothing really ...

But that is the real That is love, the admission that the poet's whole universe is just a *merle blanc*, a snowy raven, a non-existent thing which strives to live Love is the santé, the bread & dripping, the health & sanity which permeates the poem like sunlight through cedars, like whitespace through these lathery shadows of reality, these heated stones, these words Even that love & the pure intentions which go along with it cannot help but bend as they pass through the poem as light through water Such love is a very large Post-It note that the external exists, that people are still weeping beyond this solitude Love & affection are *real* & poetry leaves some aftertaste

To people who bring me drinks
to people who stay busy on my behalf
to people who feed & fondle me
to people who bring me drinks
to people who lend me things
to people who take me out
to people who bring me drinks
to people who show up
to people who help me
to people who bring me drinks
to people who love me

in some stranger way
you make me believe the poem is
what is it

Love,
Garry

Salmacis

translation for Susannah

Is this my beard
between your legs

or your warm thighs
about my beard

Nevertheless
it bristles

Is this my beard
between your breasts

or your wet boobs
about my beard

Nevertheless
it bristles

Is this your beard
between my legs

or my soggy thighs
about your beard

Nevertheless
it bristles

Ode to Soft Offices

for Alessandra

A voice like fading
vodka Knock three

times thick
yellow spirals

This proposition
lost in the wind

A scent of
stimulants

A round of
depressants

This proposition
lost in the wind

Sensuous flesh
in contextuality

Here's something
on the erotic

This proposition
lost in the wind

You are the only
one in the field

& my office
she asks

This proposition
lost in the wind

Choreograph

translation for Tara v9.2

Salomé, would you dance
over every white space

I miss you no doubt
I miss your dance more

Salomé, would you dance
over every awkward pause

There's no room for this moon
a cocoon wriggling to hatch

Salomé, would you dance
over such mistaken eggs

Butterflies are ugly
up close Just watch

Salomé, would you dance
over the canvas once more

My wings are caught in
the glass & it is crackt

Salomé, would you dance
over every white space

Optics

translation for Lisbeth

Your lights are on
(You like to watch)

Your hands are full
(You like to watch)

Your eyes are nice
(You like to watch)

Your cries are soft
(You like to watch)

Your hair is long
(You like to watch)

Your chest is big
(You like to watch)

Your face is red
(You like to watch)

Your voice is soft
(You like to watch)

You are 3 shadows
(You like to watch)

Serenade

translation for Leeta

River, prick up your
ears, the night is wet
& in Carmencita's breasts
limbs are dying of love

Limbs are dying of love

Night sings naked
across the Lions
[
  ¡O eavesdropping stone
    of Genoa!
]
Carmencita bathes her body
in wet salt & weeds

Limbs are dying of love

Whisky clear evening
stumbles upon the rooftops
Translucent streams in the lane
The whisky of your pale thighs

Limbs are dying of love

The Modern Tempo

translation for Shannon

(*Pan to the back of a black coat, soaked through with Hollywood rain machines & trembling hands in fingerless gloves*)

CHARLIE CHAPLIN: I'd really like to sit down

(*A honking stream of traffic spins the little tramp in a circle & index fingers glow through tinted glass*)

THE SUVS: Hey, asshole Outta my way

CHARLIE CHAPLIN (*sitting on the wet sidewalk along Broadway*): What a lovely spot

STARBUCKS ASSOCIATE: What's that little punk up to

(*A chocolate lab comes up to Charlie, licking his face affectionately A woman pulls away the dog in a hurry, juggling her grande latté & a screaming perambulator handle*)

MAN OUTSIDE CIBC: Hey I'm playing the spoons here Find your own turf

PERAMBULATOR (*adorably*): Waaaaaaaaaaaaaaaaaaaaaaaaaaaaaaaaaaaaaaa

(*Charlie gambols about comically in his drenched threads until he comes across a piece of white placard in a garbage can He picks it up & suddenly a dozen Safeway workers leave their picket line Fortunately, he eludes them & finds a syringe in a nearby schoolyard Pricking his finger, he writes a concise message in anemic hemoglobin & sits down again outside Starbucks*)

W.C. FIELDS: What does that say WILL DANCE FOR FOOD I oughta wring your neck I oughta strangle you with both hands

(*Charlie starts to freak out but all of a sudden the image of Edison stealing the idea of a lightbulb appears just above his itchy scalp*)

CHARLIE CHAPLIN: Eureka, the vacuum people

(*Charlie flips the placard over & writes HELP WANTED in his thinning blood When the manager turns his head, he slips it into the front window of Starbucks*)

FRANCHISE MANAGER: Hey you, get the hell out

(*Charlie won't take no for an answer He mimes his enthusiasm to serve coffee & join their fine organization & Chaplins out his empty pockets, pointing frantically to the HELP WANTED sign*)

FRANCHISE MANAGER (*whispering*): Well we are an equal-opportunity employer

CHARLIE CHAPLIN (*pulling out a tarnished Star of David & a First Nations bird totem from Taiwan*): I gots what it takes

FRANCHISE MANAGER (*tossing a sickly green smock in his face*): We'll give you a trial today If you do good then we'll talk further Just don't screw up … & take that damn hat off

(*Charlie promptly tosses his bowler hat out the door He gleams with pride as it is raining unemployed statisticians in bowler hats on this particular day*)

CHARLIE CHAPLIN (*raising invisible bowler*): & how are you today

SHAUGHNESSY SOCCER MOM: Cold & wet I'll have a no whip non-fat double short lightly massaged slightly stirred decaf latté in the shape of a cumulus cloud & I mean like rose petals Also a tall Italian

CHARLIE CHAPLIN (*looking around for a tall swarthy fellow*): We are all out We only have one short Jew

(*Charlie kisses her adagio con passione & con amore verismo Her perambulator twitches in time with his tiny moustache*)

CHARLIE CHAPLIN (*pinching*): & did you want a pinch of cinnamon with that

(*Outside, her blue merle sheltie is anxious & rather appalled She races back out with her no whip non-fat double short etc*)

CHARLIE CHAPLIN: & how are you today

SELF-IMPORTANT PRICK (*tapping foot & watch*): Let's speed this kissing contest up already I'm late for work Give me the usual Here's my coffee card & here's my MasterCard & I want to put more money on my coffee card & make it snappy why don't you

CHARLIE CHAPLIN (*wistful, longing for the era before talkies*): Just a quick peck then

(*Charlie swipes the prick's card & sparks shoot out of the swiper His entire client history lolls madly out of the mouth of debits & credits & Charlie tears off the little squares of print one at the time, slipping in puddles of boiling coffee & hitting his head on the bean-grinder innumerable times*)

FRANCHISE MANAGER: Attention la boisson …
(*A leggy waif played by Paulette Goddard lounges on a bit of newsprint outside the location location, her eyes darting a butane flame of desperation & cunning*)

CHARLIE CHAPLIN (*dreamily*): I do have this job Maybe one day we could shack up together

FRANCHISE MANAGER: That little quiff I'm just waiting for the day she troubles a customer

WAIF (*crossing legs anxiously in the metal door frame*): I'm pissing my drawers

FRANCHISE MANAGER: You have to buy something The washrooms are for customers only

[Hours later …]

(*Pan to Charlie's crossed eyeballs & rollicking tongue Hours of latté & cappucino construction & meaningless repartée have driven him neon-green with insanity Also an undesirable has just jumped bail & has methodically planted his stash into packets of Mutrasweet Charlie tries to calm down with a cup of coffee but finds his double coke decaf to be a little strong for his system*)

CHARLIE CHAPLIN (*to parking meter*): & how are you today

PARKING METER: Click clack click clack click clink clack

CHARLIE CHAPLIN: S'all good no worries

WAIF: Hey mista spare a loon for some coffee & hence the taboo loo

CHARLIE CHAPLIN (*convulsing & twitching at the word "loon" & yanking coat hanger out of his unzipped trousers*): Eureka, the vacuum people

WAIF: ¿Whafuh?

CHARLIE CHAPLIN (*jimmying the parked SUV the old-fashioned way*): & how are you today

CAR ALARM: Huzza Don't touch me there it's not fair Whookookachooooo

(*Pedestrians walk by & shrug & mutter about the noise*)

DALMATION: Thanks for letting me outta there, mister tramp

CHARLIE CHAPLIN: You're quite welcome my sensitive eloquent friend

(*The Franchise Manager sends out a Starbucks Associate to inform Charlie he is being downsized*)

STARBUCKS ASSOCIATE: Now you're firing me too!

FRANCHISE MANAGER: Yup

CHARLIE CHAPLIN (*reading an instruction manual in the glove compartment & getting the ignition going with the emergency paper clip*): Storm the snowpea palace Storm the snowy obelisk Storm the green bastille

WAIF (*caressing Charlie supportively*): Will you marry me Chump I mean Chuck I mean Chuck

(*Charlie floors it, frapping the ebony SUV through glass The Franchise Manager bounces ragdollishly off the dent-resistant panels & gets his comeuppance in the bean grinder The last thing he sees is something very brown & green although the airbag is smothering his last words*)

WAIF: Yipeeeeeee But I really have to pee now honestly

CHARLIE CHAPLIN (*asterisks in his eyes*): Knock yerself out

WAIF (*a trickle then a flush then a dab of pink liquid soap*): What's the use of even trying

CHARLIE CHAPLIN: Let's scram, baby

(*A collapsing Siren hits his head a number of times & Paulette Goddard, disguised as Marion Pauline Levy, props him up for the long journey to Whistler & other portentous adventures*)

CHARLIE CHAPLIN: When we getting to Florida Everybody's talking at me, I don't hear a word they're saying …

WAIF: There there

(*As they walk off into the setting sun they are mistaken for protesting students & the police decide to bash potential dissent out of their heads, utilizing only rubber bullets & gentle edges of pavement*)

AUTHORITY #1: Calling in a 711

AUTHORITY #2: If they're not hockeymad they're protesting Suharto or Mugabe or the Olympics or some shit

AUTHORITY #1: Tim Hortons

AUTHORITY #2: Yah

Sigh/Press

translation for Roy

Press
[Water is bottled]

Press
[Liquid crystal display]

Press
[Form submitted]

Remember
[¿Do not click this box in future?]

Press
[It is now safe to shut off your system]

The One Damn Time

translation for George

Nothing but language
that speaks for itself

Here I am in the nosebleeds
7th inning, thinking of Jack

& who is the pitcher anyway &
boy these pitchers are pricey

clamatosized cans for 5 clams
& I'm not even thinking of you

cold eternal
flower girl

cuz literature is thought
now, or on second thought

later I might catch a pop
fly or is it out of the

park Nooo, nothing Language
alone That speaks for itself

Attached

translation for George

I do not abhor those attached
but I never look at them

I reside like an avatar
in this virtual reality

just behind Safeway
I turn around &

even Safeway is missing
where I stroll buying safes

imagining what if I ever
take that breadth course

& become like this stale
bread? O best to give up

get certified & cease
reading, like librarians

starving cooks who heat
up no instant delicacies

keeping inventory for this
discreet advert for Safeway

smiling at The Other, taking
our repetitive strain injury

down an aching tunnel of love
reminding this isn't a party

someone has to fuck chi chi
someone has to hold the sign

Once I opened an attachment
& now I never look at them

Supernova

translation for Jamie

The hyperbolic supernova
is about to hit the earth

erasing leaden etchings
of legalized profundity

Some body really sucked
monkeys & another spilt

immortal brandy & soda
down the front of Poetry

I learned the hard way
supernovae never never

smile in photographs
while crossing borders

& never existed outside
our flat earth societies

No fakir climbed higher
than systemic debunking

& no poet existed without
Official Party paperwork

In spite of our telekinesis
balls still fell into holes

with unfathomable sadness
& no light could escape

limits of our imagination
or surpass Ontario suburbs

or edges of our dullness
except for Leonard Cohen

Garbage Disposal

translation for Blog

Electronic lips switch to SHIFT
upon the prematurely premature

blabby head that would turn to
mush had it nutrients of gruel

but no one listens to poetry
over that truck backing up

hocking boxes stuffed with
not really paying attention

to purchase state of the Art
systems without spell check

TABbing through second life
blithely unminding the first

but no one listens to poetry
over that stenchsome racket

bouncing balls back & forth
like metaphors about love

referencing this poem
to cover a drinks bill

as long & dreary & national
as a prairie in depression

but no one listens to poetry
over the brain linked fence

like lyrics on hold, whatever
is not the awaited utterance

that wealth of knowledge
more expensive than free

sniffing Proper Names out of
paper held by blogritic hands

but no one listens to poetry
over pollution of gadgetalia

Prickly Pear

translation for Daphne

Wild salmon

¡How well you look
in the half-light!

A dream of you
I saw you tomorrow
in the house of Joy

You were weeping
A wounded cherry
clung to life

A dream of you
between me & the
prickly pear

¡How well you look
biting the wind!

Not only Attis
knows this pain

Unexplained

Hybridity

translation for Wayde

Red tits of the sun
Blue tits of the moon

Part cotton
Part lycra
Part spandex
Part polyester

Part shadow

Wash separately

Dear Jack,

We live in such an age of interruption there is more time spent on the particulars of getting together than actual meetings Once the poem had an aim, an ambition of sorts, a confirmation of see you there on such & such at so & so & now it just shivers &

shakes on the page Interruption teases & tickles It bristles with language How many A hundred, a thousand, a million eyes & hips & chests & cunts & cocks ask for it to bristle

Even if we can't get together, the poem & language go on talking Things are disclosed & revealed in places where nobody is Language outgrows any *mens rea*, any evidence of intent I didn't mean it really That was language talking We were both a kind of misleading question mark Even those polite requests for reassurance do you love me don't you want to go to bed with me do you love me sound abhorrent beside the altercosm of language which is naturally dirty The very real pause or clause is a threat to shatter that beautiful loneliness so necessary to poetry So we go to bed together without a word while language whispers from dusty aisles & pissy alleyways & sore asses

It strokes the ego of our loneliness & gives it shape Can you hear it thrum in your head yet, thick & salty as a verbial sea I feel I fished you out, a friend said I needed to be fished out The integrity of language is reinforced by its betrayal of the burning bleeding weeping world outside the word Someone is outside the thick mauve loneliness can you hear them knocking Tell them I don't want to see them Just us tonight, Jack

In poems, we sleep with everything relative, Ancient Greek daughters hidden up in the Attic & tall striking hermaphrodites & yes fishes too It is inevitable I will be fished out The phone will ring & that will become part of the dream we are chewing on A rush of ideas will surround the intruder & make a god of it, err the interruption I mean, mere cheeks of ideas you can't quite catch or kill or clean or clack, just a glimmer in the purple wave

Poets often take revenge & kill the living in poems, to prove they can Yes at some point that knock at the door or telephone call will be impossible to ignore & a finality will enter But no one ever dies in a poem I am lying of course When you love someone, it happens But tonight is for us Tonight, let's get misled together Tonight, let's get our hands dirty Tonight, do you have a spare shovel Tonight, let's rob the grave together

On the other hand, must dash—time, money & all the rest …

Y(ours),
Garry

Soy un Perdedor

translation for Jessica

Loneliness is a perfectly pink
conch shell on a grey afternoon

Deep inside her nacreous cunt
I hear an ocean full of garbage

The hairy nostrils of heroes
sensitize her shivering thighs

Deep inside her nacreous cunt
I hear a woman stuffed with soy

The soggy beards of heroes
hang about her, glistening

Deep inside her nacreous cunt
I hear an old boner recharge

Full of bear gall the heroes
are strapping on strap-ons

Deep inside her nacreous cunt
swollen ankles go varicose

Full of black piss the heroes
whack off tables for more

Loneliness is a perfectly blue
conch shell on a grey afternoon

Bad Timing

for Sian

Want to have a stiff one

– It is 11:47 Paradise
passes on the Granville
bus I sprint after
unreliable antennae &
my poppy drops into
the puddled gutter
You did ask

Want to have a stiff one

– It is 11:58 Paradise
is gold in the men's
room You did ask

Want to have a stiff one

– It is 12:19 Paradise
is cold warmed up by
my own hands You
did not refuse

Want to have a stiff one

– It is 12:34 Paradise
is bold in that fierce
embrace You did
not refuse

Want to have another

– It is 12:47 Paradise
has started to rain
again Want to come
under my umbrella

You did not ask
& you did refuse

One Night Stand

translation for Goh Poh

I found her downtown
not a ring on her finger
but she had a man

It was hockey night
& everyone was inside
Street lights were snuffed
& joints were lit up

In the horniest corners
I touched her sleeping breasts
& suddenly they opened
like flasks of absinthe

Her synthetic skirt
bellowed in my ear
like some authentic beast
brought down by 8 rifles

There seemed more trees
behind the strange haze
as a sunset of dogs
yelped for help

Past the blackberries
full of freeway snipers
beneath her matted hair
I dug a pit of silicon

I took off my shirt
She took off her skirt
Me, the automatic belt
She, the sweatshop of
underthings

Tubes & jars know
no skin so fine &
glasses of cognac
don't glimmer so

Her thighs escaped
like wild salmon
half cooked with fever
half frozen with waste

That night I drove
the bumpiest of roads
in a brand new Land
Rover full of leather

Gentlemen mustn't repeat
the things in her mouth
The gleam of her credit
card swiped my lips shut

& maybe her Maybelline
was smeared out of town
while the air beat off
a long song of make-believe

Be yourself I said
A legitimate prick
I gave her a few bucks
& a bag of catnip

I didn't feel
like falling for her
since she had a man
& said I had first crack
when I found her downtown

Pub Night

translation for Lisa

The library is quiet
with no one inside it

We talked in the cold
You were very pretty

The library is quiet
with no one inside it

I attempted an exit
Angels drove me back

The library is quiet
with no one inside it

We touched in the cold
You were very pretty

The library is quiet
with no one inside it

A hundred voices
pump up the volume

The library is quiet
with no one inside it

I tried to make an exit
Angels drove me home

The library is quiet
with no one inside it

Dear Jack,

Even the beautiful funny people have come to feel like obstructions, exhausting me with very small talk or making dates & appointments for me which get in the way of what we have Here, studying your blank dead face, gleaming in the dark before our last rendezvous, I feel a sense of rejection & betrayal in the air

There is some demi-urge at the back of my throat, asking that we just be friends We have to stop meeting like this Yet I know the moment I slam the window shut on your mealy fingers these keys will no longer depress with the same character in mind, that pens will grow chains & grow thirsty & any attempt to talk will taste like a polluted lake upon any tongue Have I left you alone for too long Have I neglected you Can't we just enjoy these final moments together You (& me both) always spoil things

October is here & what harvest to reap I peer into giant cardboard boxes full of pumpkins for your huge head (since size does matter), thinking to scalp you & heat up your hidden seeds But now I drop my knife to the floor, nervous in the attempt, in the thought of it The leaves have been late to fall & I am happy the summer has lingered for our sake, as if all this live talk should keep leaves on trees in a stubborn state of green

Now there is some other beauty & it threatens to tear us apart, limb by limb, page by page Not the props of love nor the adulation of strangers I have said there is a feeling in the air I can hear them cutting you up in front of me but I dare not look They are giving you a lobotomy to make you smile They are ripping up your membrane They are taking your eyes

No Jack, I don't want to see it I can't bear to see them dissect you I will hold you in my mind as I want to in my arms, as I would the others if I could Tomorrow I will wake up & the trees will be naked & I won't remember much of our talk in the twilight but I imagine you will be about, all the same

Love,
Garry

Guzzle of the Terrible Wanderthirst

translation for Alison

I want the essence of wet
I want the remnants of breath

I want the night to shut my eyes
I snatch the flower from my heart

I want the soft echo of feet
& a camel coat of shadow

I want candelabra from eyes
& such insistence from a nose

I can watch the train of twilight
pull away & watch noon arrive

I can stomach the ancient jar
of jealousy & even lick the ladle

But do not look at me that way
since I am quite unslaked

Leave me in a shadow of thirst
but do not look at me that way

Guzzle of Love in the Backseat Heading Backeast

translation for Farrell

Every evening in this city
love expires, every evening
Every evening, water rests
in the soft ebb of reflection

A glaucous-winged gull
glides beneath the moist
teeth of loitering clouds
tragically omening rain

Then the rapid beating
of a rose hummingbird
will never be heard
will never be heard

Every evening violet twilight
meets the lowing of a cloud
& a wounded love expires
like a crocus in the snow

Guzzle of the Quick Needlework

translation for Marjory

Then leave without a word
leave, but leave me that word

a tremble of cherry blossoms
in the dark treble of March

The sonata of needle & thread
leaves stalk & aching flower

All night in the suburb
my eyes, like two labs

All night in the suburb
a strange aftertaste

Sometimes the wind
is an ersatz flower

sometimes the pluck
of flapping lapels

The sonata of needle & thread
leaves stalk & aching flower

They will come to cut
the silence of grass

as a ladybird on the glass
rouses a sleeping silverfish

But leave without a word
leave it alone on my coat

Guzzle of Emerald Leavings

translation for Carmel

There is a sable rainbow
upon the railing of twenty-seven terraces

The winter of a single palm
could never survive such heights

Where are you going, where?
There is a sky of one million
windows Why has the rock
dove come to peck at mine?

Iridescent

It hurts the beak It hurts
to peck sable rainbows in
stone, or the rusted grey
railing of twenty-seven terraces

Love, come to roost
but leave your green
winter

Guzzle of the Blackberry Sleep

translation for The Railway

I want to sleep the sleep of black
berries by the resonance of dead railways
I want to sleep the sleep of that imperfect
aria, to leave that dark note upon lips

Do not say the dead are not bruised
that still they thirst for light & water
Do not say you have given yourself
for a single taste of obsidian sleep

I want to sleep only for a moment
a moment, a minute, a century
Yet say I have not died
that I live among brambles
that I devour rain & dust
that I am a shadow of sleep

Then kiss me carefully with your dark lips
Then squeeze me to death with your fists
but taste me for the itinerary of eternity
but taste me for the itinerary of eternity

Since I want to sleep the sleep of black
berries by the resonance of dead railways
since I want to live the death of every
perception, to gleam among thorns

Guzzle of the Shattered Vanity

translation for Sandra

Upon the antique vanity
whose mirror had met

disaster, I thought
of Spring alone &

felt the body of night
flooded with blossoms

The body of night
became a stellar

field & my hands
white nightingales

Upon the antique vanity
they beat their wet wings

& with a satisfying creak
the mirror was full of ink

Mr. Gottago

translation for Barb

Wouldn't it be sweet
to die on Morton St

as Virginia Creeper
creeps about us

to sit in the View
& listen to the Feed

beside a honking
V
of SUVs

to write each night
in cobwebbed writ

as Virginia Creeper
creeps about us

to sit in the View
& listen to the Feed

& wouldn't it be neat
to die on Morton St

beneath a honking
V
of SUVs

Book of Strains

with words by
Garry Thomas Morse

Improvisation on a Phrase by Rimbaud

"Genius music misses our desire"
A traditional counter
Point of conversation. The bird
On the quiet balcony of crap translates
Whistles the wind. The sea
Is solitary down the street. Meaning
Less as glockenspiel
Not even a xylophone. Resist
Touch on the quiet balcony of crap. Counter
Point of conversation. Unorthodox
Conversion. Bird, jukebox. Real
Music

A Valentine

Hearts move through the thorough
Fare, *obbligato.* Hearts
In hands. Visual
Poetry. Bad
Poetry. The
Bluff, *ad libitum*
Is a long way down
But tonight the hearts are
Definite. Stop moving

Fugue

Silly
How a little song and a little voice
Lacks words and threatens our poetry
We bunch together and in
Visibly dream of brunch. Hope to
Meet. Rain threatens. Sloth. Terror
Race up and down stairs
Believe nothing

Orfeo

Take them then. Orpheus
does not need them to sing. Hell
Is there. Music
At the bottom of this
Lost
Obstreperousness
Eurydice
Is solid. Rock. Yesterday's
Meat. Eat
Nothing. The infernal
Is the lap of the lap behind the lap
Hell is this:
The eternal complaint department. Despair
Gum in hair or works
Only a bed of
Music to sleep in

Song of a Gaol Bird

Nothing escapes
The pinch bottle of my body. Birds
Mating and murdering and being
Murders. A collection of nesting
Materia. Nothing escapes
Each branch is closed
I
Rattle for attention
With an injured limb

Zero Sum

The size is zero
We wear the decade
Upon our backs, wear
Out many exotic
Uniforms. We
Fill out the card
With a number of
Zeroes, or our
Declaration is
Denied. Last year
We watched zero
The object is zero

Monday: The Empty Gazebo

A face, exquisitely equine
A nose, by no means aquiline
Clipped and clopped
By the empty gazebo
"Change," I asked
Change for a
Free band?"
"No," she moaned
"The Sunday
Music has stopped
You could not hear them. I am
Veering about the green"
She pulled
Away with the screech
Of a distinct chalk

Bummer

The word is mimEEEsis
Of a mating hummingbird
Of a mulching summer
Of a meddling sum
Of mothers coming
Understanding is not enough
The syllable was getting up there. A flock
Of summers flooding the sky
A flock of summers

The Poet Reclining

Beneath the purple haze
Holding his throat. The horse and pig
Dog graze upon green
Motionless as dream
Do they also dream
Outside the frame, the
Sleeper has been soundly
Shot. He is dying from
Lack of poetry, from
Paint beneath the purple haze
                        That horse and pig
Dog freeze
graze upon green

Ghost Song

Before the cock
Crows
Before the cock
Rose
Mean
(we ran into a bewilderness
to elude predators, the mean)
Before the cock
Cocks
(show me where the lightning is, no
don't tell me, deep in the seamy soil)
In love. In love. In love. The
Rose
Cock
(as if nothing were left
but an echo in love)

Artificial Turf War

The invasion was a big
Obsession. A huge success
Mission accomplished. Game
Over. Major Havoc
Jumped over a green
Asterisk. And some
Body had taken the escape
Pod. And we
We were not afraid to split up by the
Wire and face the same enemy, the same
Love

Sonata for a Chair and a Table

The sound of words falling from our mouths are not
Crumbs. Nothing
Is less a sonata
          But this chair
                    this table
                              called
Acquire properties
                                        assume positions
Share a type of music
Words arrange things. Make
                                                  names
That will forever hurt them
                                                    I
By this divine signature am a table
Talk to the chair
Fill it with song a delicious lack of sitters
And we
Who in a similar model of music
Are easily moved and dusted
Under
We can swallow our own
In a similar moment of music
Help the dead move

Paranoia

A fiddle is shadowing me

In the public house of the world
The same tune and not this
Self-same tune
For the paying public playing it

It shadows me with unspeakable scorn

And my favourite organ fears
Abandonment from the same tune. They
In the public house in the world
Fear its lack of abandonment

Or it looks just like the silent
Complaint in my gut. In the corner
Of eyes just like theirs, a shadow
Music

A Book of Strains

Coming to a point, the lovers
   Opposite   pull apart like hands
Wringing and washing furiously. No love
Is a word in the ocean a dizzy
Voyeurism of the lapping
Edge. Two can emerge exhausted
Thinking what to say stupid
Breathing hard
Coming to a point, or the end of
Ink
Making the messiest of
Farewells
Meanwhile, we loved
And the rest of us
Remains on shore. A
Dish of ink

The Rent Annals of Billy The Kid

I

Where were you when you heard
(Panting in the cool sunlight after)
The frontier was an infinite link. Is. Follow it where
Ever it go. He was content to live in a cup. He once
Said he never saw a moose could gallop. I said wait
Till it win the Kentucky Derby. Then I spat into the
Magic of an *articulate spittoon.* Thrilled by the thorny
Circumcision of my obsidian pajamas before Billy
Gave me no arrowhead. And not a word of a
Fib, he used the old reach
Around technique

More contortedly, I heard through the Wire
Reluctant Billy sucked off the Grim Reaper

In Indian summer, you get mighty thirsty. Deep
In the gulch, merrily belching off the glare made
Gloomy. Even the S.O.S. of the Morse dried up
In the dust. What went down. Looking Moyle
Horse in the mouth, a sacrificial prose
Purpling
Symbolish. Who knew

II

A chocolate bar wrapper. Gold in the
Clang of his nibblies. *Chalcopyrite*, the fancy
Man name for the gold of a fool. We ate it
The same
At midnight
The collage party
Was a scream in the dark
Without ice cream. Did the words
Go wild, Billy? The dark chocolate
Of Billy, unwrapped in the closet
Game. Tasting almost
The same
Among the clanging hangers
Billy invented the Internet
And gambled it away
Tomorrow
                The handjobs of heroes
                                                                        are often edited
Out
      by the news
                                  Billy,   Billy,   Billy,   they said
and tomorrow
                        Billy

Did not have a gun in his pocket
Did not even blow up the buildings

And he never ever got to Montréal

Billy was a collage
Left on the coffee
Table, barely
Tabula rasa
Among the clanging
digitals of naked
Billys

III

He had charisma and rococco machismo
Stretched out at the edge of inexistent river
Where we versed awhile
"Snap out of it. It ain't
Real. The horizon I mean
Is only a curveball of your
Eyeball getting pitched"
"Maybe," he said. "But no
Body likes to hear it"
And his pants stopped
And my pants stopped
They were so unreal
And big trouble
Like a hot dog
Running away with four
Balls in its
Mouth

IV

Percival and Sheriff
Trotted up to Billy
Warned him off a
Type of penetration
reminding him don't
Mix milk and meat
Indians are Indians
And Jews sure ain't
Cowpokes. Already
Framed him. The
Next night he waited
Under the stairs, his
Left hand just
                    itching
                              jumping
                 from
                      behind

V

Billy The Kid in a Dijon field, clean breathing
Ethanol. Only the barn
Owl knowing Billy the
Double agent
                    working his ass off for Colonel Mustard
        who
                who
Who knew
Billy The Kid
Drove a
Bug

VI

Pa pa pa
Paaaaa pa pa pa
Still smoking in the
Incubator two hundred fifty
Years later, the registered
Hand that popped
Papageno and
Papagena in the
Who who
            (you did not look so immortal at the Chinese
              laundromat. You took another swig of Club Soda
                and threw in three gallons of überwhite detergent)
I know Billy
You never did
Your own
Laundry
I know Billy
They found the
Kernel and a whole
Continent of butter
In urban arteries
I know Billy
In the library

VII

You say cicadas dip through the desert
Sipping chocolate mirages
I say sick-aw-daws
With a broken
A. And
Guinevere, wondering
Who you have to fuck to
Free Billy
On the safe side
Fucking everyone
(Hell, Billy did)
Dark chocolate heads
Snapping between her
Teeth

VIII

Billy was a Titian
Groomed in crisis
Got a mare in trouble
Could barely concentrate on the
Cards in front of him. Christ
Asked him not to leave
Town after the game
He begged the Morse
For more time before
He yelped for help
"All I gots is riding
On the eighth race"
But the giant clock
Invited him to the
Shitkicker's Ball
And dancing too
Close, I whistled
Run Billy run. The
Race is fixed. Don't
Miss the last bus
Like I might've
But that little
Puke could
Never take
No hint

IX

The Left
Handed Gun
Was an epic of dressing
Wars. A classic. We
Fiddled around while
Salad fields burned
Love. Pouring
Out like oil and
Vinegar. Yet hard. A
Diamond commercial
Dewatering lakes
Going bling bling
In Billy's brain
Whenever he
Mouths off
If a diamond
Felt off the
Back of a fuck
Where would you
Pierce me. With
Percival peeping through
Unsimilied cypresses
Sexy as death
Here
        and here and
                                        here
So hard
You kill
Billy
The Kid

X

Billy The Kid
This is difficult
Billy The Kid
I got your back
Remember the time we chewed the phat
Music of cicadas and munched the magic
Rug together. Skinny dipping in the dark
Freudian chocolate factories
And then you fixed my printing
Problem and I tore you a new
One and you got real sore
Billy The Kid
(You are wanted more
Than you are wanted)
Just stop your groin
Groanin' young
Whipper

Hands Dirty

Art
Flicks through your
Eyes
And your tongue darts dragon
Fire upon antique flagons It
Is the levelling of your look the
Taking in that
Attracts
As if
Through the classic ocean ((I))
Is still listening
To that rapid
Survey of
Form and
Line even as you stretch to put something
Back there is
A movement in the urbane
Jungle
And in this labyrinth of
Rolling
Things
Thrills

Got
Designs. More than
Mere glare. The cut of
Cloth cheap
Labour in a   distance
            Traces ambiguous speech of your
Shape. It is not always
Inside. It
Is inter
Active with
Painted
Fingers
Painting
Tearing. It
Is winter
Ized. You
Just have to
Touch just one of
Them
Words in the
Dark to
Know and
Watch them grow. Giant C
Monkeys of
Desire and a
Whale of a
Gloss

Language
Is
Immediate
Heat
Loss
Of the four
Play of word
Play or
            Flaccid
                        Banter
More
Sudden
Fuck
Behind

And she laughed
And God asked
Why she laughed
And God knows
Was not her reply
But for a moment
Metaphor made her
Feel like a whore
And these lines
Scrolled on and
On through her
Mind and after
Time she didn't
Mind and the
Idea had a life
Of its own she
Learned and
Wanted and
Wanted and
In the desert
Of ands she
Soon anded

It

It is the opposite of a social
    Why we are here   She
Studies the canvas and gets
It a little bit. It. And why are you
Here. I
Came with some colossal
Calamari on a
Floor of anemone
And heard the
Purple Conch
Of your
Sex
And we didn't eat there again. Fresh
Canvas. And the dream
Refreshed. Tide
Whiter than white that ala-
Bastard inside a
Flower of the sea
Stinging. Fresh
Meat to
Eat or
Ream, turning
Colours, ink
Deep

                              A
Word. The way you
Swallow it or hold it
Back
          And through the proverbial
Blue streaks of
Yes
        Zoom through another bill
Board the
                    Letters
              Encounters and
                            Two
                                     Fingered
                                                       Whistles
                    In the echo of after
Hours that clutch and
Clip of inebriated
Heels almost
Pulpable
                 Chalking up charcoal
Upon a palette of
Papery
Wet

Thought. A
thought softer than
Words where I
Bristle between your
Digits and spoon out your
Brains without the moon
Madness dances. Semi a
Sleep the dozing
Cock is anxious to
Wake me without a
Thought. You stir to life
Useless
Thought
Unless
Unless
Unless with soft you
Translate softly into
Lieder with your
Omni
Potence
Of
Lips

There is a lot of pain in
Paint
And no
Poetry and
Writing your
Name in the sand and
Fretting over amperrr
Sands
Between the cheeks of a do
Able
Muse
A lot to losing imaginary
Numbers to
Ghosts of
Lovers
And
Jealousy a h e l l u v a lot of
Pain in a
Brief history of slow
Indifferent
Hours
Of not coming
Back to
Bed

How many more arguments
And conversations end like

This

You started it. No
You. With that
Thing you always do

Always was the
Tongue got me in
Trouble. And that
Mouth on you

Blazes in your
Eye with no small
Idolatry. The shape of a
Fist squeezes tube in this
Lost
Spurt of viridian on
White

Then the apparition of
Morning
Breath Warm as
Imaginary animals in those
Caves of Lascaux how many
Thousands of years ago the self
Same heat and desire the
Same fucking
Argument

Hallucinatory Elegies

for Jack Spicer

i

This note-
book for one buck (a
real loonie) is the last
virgin here
                    I open you
                                        Pathetically, I
punctuate. My limitations
to make a point

       Since, there's always been a woman
last night, the one with her   white
            boot a-tapping to fiddle & flute

or the Spanish flirt in passage
        sashaying the long raven hair
                    of her beer commercial tragedy
   unzipping
                      some parked
                                            dénouement

But the timer
                      continues to tick. The
              hell's wings are nearly done   I open
the freezer & the Jamaican style ginger
     beer is much much cooler. Cold
as poetry means less than
hot. Sometimes I leave
a poem on the stove
& it sets off my smoke
                                    alarm
                                                  far too sensitive
        Even inconstant faucets
        can burn

Poetry, how can you be so cold
         or breed fevers when you chill
                                                       the intellect
Were you hiding in those five pints
last night? You know, I find

refrains are suggestive
are whispers in the sea. Can we
even trust in them, cold
externals
to our senses shocked—
by a touch
on the shoulder
(of glass)
Settle down:
adagio
ma non troppo e molto cantabile
the story of my life, or so she writes
"An old man plays
poorly. Listen. There's
the pain ..."

I follow dark ellipses like those into the page's distance
that terrify some neat souls
They eclipse my near-
sighted vision
& lead me on a late-night quest
for that crowded
tavern of the soul

I down another. O my ear
envelopes you, my sweet engine of
fire. My ear envelops you
parenthetically (
still at home with Beethoven
's piano, violin & violoncello. A
nebulous ménage à trois
a triptych of instruments

The women last night
begin to dance together
belting out
"Hotel California"
when
imperative

ii

I'm nothing but iambs, bro-
ken un/breathed ink-
lings. Whatever
is touched
turns to gold, even
fleshy rumps
Everything
I am touched
by poetry
a different curse
I
spit
lyrical along the streets
of old loves, long dead

Lyrically, to stretch the legs
of language, to lie
before the tweezers & microfiche
can catch you in the
magic act

It be more honest to talk ugly
or wrongly. Like a murder
of pundits squawking
Jobs! Jobs! Jobs!

The hotel face has deteriorated
During
our after-dinner nightcap, the tourist
view is blotted out by scaffolding
Black water
we have to stop
meeting like this

iii

Might we mutter about magic
Now. The tricks of language
line up across the page
Tchaikovsky gets burlesque
laughing, babbling, burbling
The tricks of language want
to tie you up, to get tied up. They are hand-
woven by local fakirs in the dark
as long as they have the nerve to talk.

Black ink on my right pinky
utterly smudged
The sea out there
is singing
I feel dirty, listening
to this ditty

I loved golliwogs
Because they were
more beautiful, more anatomically correct-
ed than a topheavy Barbie to play with
wrapped in pink cardboard & plastic
But that prototype, that model
lives in the factory reject
of innumerable poetic
devices

Today, Beatrice would
talk a lot about mutual
funds. Dante would have
a better hat. He would say
she seemed to be the daughter
of someone better than a banker
& they would. Unconditionally

It's magic. The Irish fly
that buzzed iridescently
into Mider's ears
until he was aggravated
to sleep

He rolled
over & forgot
every other
voice

I'm in love with a counter-
tenor"

You would

iv

Time will tell
on me
I was looking
for some doll with deep
pockets, in order to hold
special poetry collections
the size of coffee tables

As if the poem. That pretty
boy drunk who rolls crumpled
poems under tables & begs for
glasses of water, rough sketching
in scribbles & Greek part-
i-cles & partisssssipples

Time is sittting in my pocket, un-
strapped. Hey wait for me, my lovely century!
(Sic) your rabid team of woolly hypocrite
diggers on my iambic bones. Dia-
ghost me for osteopoesis already!

Time, Indian-bartered for Art

I keep talking to God because I
believe
coincidences
& benevolence
are a sign of the time

Time I wear black. Verseperly
I smell the pagan stain

of my own blood—
(*istoria*—a means of inquiry)
is after all, an-
Other story
I begin to black out. The
cannibal spirit
is sizing you up
If you dare answer
I will eat you for brunch
over-easy

Time will not be killed
without a fight
Time will
kill us in self-
defence

Shrug. I declare my shrug

This is not getting any better
This is the same damned work
This is unfinished business, etc

v

I think
I am writing music
for the trained ear. She
& the rest stretch & yawn. She
is outgrowing some great power
that never existed
It's all in your head
sweetheart
head
sweet
heart

I walk
I walk along the street [let's say Larch
because it's so delicious to say my stomach
lurches along Larch & wouldn't it be neat
to die on Morton St]

I walk. This time I might just catch her. I
am erect & ready for this literary crime—
the strap of her expensive imaginary bag
snaps
words
fall
out

I walk past. There is pleasure
in such passages. Then, a woman
whispers
"I believe in the manifest"

I think. She is listening over there
in front of the black water. I can see
tides if I like, & the grey rock she barn-
a-cles to
I can even see bare trees. A
woman calls them Irish lyres

I walk past. Flashes. A
promise of pleasure from
underneath a pink slicker
& tangerine umbrella
Belly buttons in winter
drenched with raindrops. Don't
you get cold
"Don't worry, I'll keep
us *both* warm, hunbun"

I walk. I just want to talk
My imprints are purely psychical

The rain
won't stop
falling

I walk
I think. Heart
pumps to head
I go on
walking ...)

vi

My lucky #. Blah
blah. Blah blah. The end
of art as we pretend to know
it. Blah. Blah. Very Ovid
          of ya, to try (*essai*) to write
                                        nothing
then to whip out that metre/no
teacher, anything but the metre!
                                      No-
thing is growing a very long
                                  Knows

Blah blah
blah blah
I am full of gall, heavier
than bloated sea-
gulls after a breakfast
                          of twelve
                                  star
                                     fish

   "You hate my guts, don't you"

What was manifest
has become sad
digest—
        postmodern
         belch
            a grow-
         ling
            cod/fish
beaten to death
in a pale dinghy
           DUH DUH
               DUH DUH

vii

Add flour
        & shortening

I've never been happier
talking non/sense with you
Even the superficial dedication
has gotten phat between rests
                                                        Blub
                                                Blub
                                                      Blub

                                        lifting!
Maestro, something up-

Black water music. Something with
organs & pipes
                            by the pall of all my gall

My life is a
fugue
              It builds on
                        itself
                                      The same shit is recycled
                                      & rewound, with director's
                                      cuts, only never the same
                                      replay by the light of a
                                                                 drifting afternoon

Learn the dark art of
forgetting. Remember. Now
speed it up!

                        Repetition is not what you
think. Repetition is not. Sleep
on it. Time will tell on
it
                                        Repetition
                                         is not
                                                          Blah blah

        My life is a fugue

The Holey Grail

The Book of Gawain
The Book of Percival
The Book of Lancelot
The Book of Gwenivere
The Book of Merlin
The Book of Gal
The Book of the Return of Arthur

The Book of Gawain

1

Mariner
Listen Mariner
Healing magic
Did not help Gawain
When the king of aluminum fishers
Dived and opened up like so much seal
Bait
Riddled in the heat. Not
Healing in the heat. Nothing
Gawain could do. Nothing
Anything
There ain't no three riddles
Just an easy grail. A
Body in the
Wood. Another body
No riddle

2

Castle
Friend the game
Is still going on
Going. The opponent is in
Visible without wires and pretty
Pretty
Hear how much
And then you get lost
Forever. An old dude
Once told me there is
One. Don't ask don't
Stare too hard. You
Might be in this
Castle now
Getting additional
Credit

3

The grail is the opposite
Not using us as a cup
For the dead
Blood or horn
Of plenty, the
Poem is a poor
Pour. Words in yer
Friendly
Cups
The wild beasts in the name of Guy
Galante have their own bloody
Blood, are perilous, are
Parlous, are
Petrified

4

They used to dress up in the
Forest and hold their
Competition, mightily
Athirst, they
Chose their favourite
Colours
Cup or
Poem
And they bittered bitterly
Because there was no
Doom or poker or
Pool, just a
Game of hunt the cup or
Poem
And so they fought
And so they thought
And then a huge
Boom
And both were flushed
Out

5

In the bloody drink
(There is no currency, only
Grail credit)
A lone lingo
Sailing away with it
Self
Anonymous
Androgynous
Wander
Lust, bailing
Wire. Singing beauty hung
Over there on the wall
Rouse thyself and douse this
Character in the
Drink
Far far far

6

Still looking. No
Mind games. Poetry and song and
Magic still might meet
Around the
Corner. Some
Body and the
Government forgot to leave
This month
Money and applause
On the dresser
Somebody else, Merlin
Mutters grimly
Who saw through time

7

Subvert
Backward walking against the
Grail they groaned in the sneezing
Passage in a discount mixer of ecstasy
And
Suffering. Or slow
Imperceptible
Compromise. When rain
Becomes rain
Bow
Fuck the gold
Gawain got the trickle
Down effect
Read burning amper
Sand and ate my
Pink
Slip
I, Gawain, who misssss
Laid the grail in
misssspelling
Would, in
Lost and
Found
Unchecked

The Book of Percival

1

Fool
Killers swooping from towers at the
Scent, tearing and searing and
Renting space
Very zen. The
Vortex flushed and the
Gyre wireless
In the trees a brief
Movement. Fool
Killers perched in the limbs
Gnawing at tender
Vitals. Poor
Little boy in the wood
Working late

2

The forest felt desert when he
Turned his back. On
What, old
Knock on wood. The
Forest felt desert. No more
Leaves. And how old
Is he and did it make a
Sound. Break the
Veil in fashion and
Does it
Sell

3

"Ship of fools" was a
Discursive artifact. We had clung to
Absence of an oak
Wine for so long. "There
Is no support to tie us to"
A love. A body. Some
Body has to bail out the
Department. Some
Body has to bail
Out
"Fool," they yelled at the
Back of his reputation
Still elbow
Deep up that
Equine
Ass

4

There must have been a common
Room for his armour to get
Nicely laid. Some
Body is sleeping in there, some
Certifiable diaspora
Told the wood
And before the soup of
Heroes had dinged, the
Knights of the table
Ushered him
Off
And his armour could be
Put down again
For thirty seconds

5

What are you doing here
I have never seen you so
Lucid. Are you going to
Get smashed. This is a
New program. Translation
"Bitch" "slut" "fierce"
Can confuse the
Lucid. And they
Suck the fucken
Life outta ya

6

Then milk and meat were the
Blood of blood. And all the
Oppositional magic was
Tardy. I have a note from my
Note, sang the little birch, a note
Getting particular. And the
Horse was served with a post
Colonial lemon muffin
in the centre. And the
Ass was safely tucked away
Fool, they chanted to be
Controversial, but in
Fact they were
More than
Hungry

7

You are maybe the one
Who can show me the
Mirror
Sitting with nothing to
Shout
A flirtation in the background and an
Ode to passion
Aggression
Spillage
"Fool" covered in guana. All
Silence and
White noise
Getting older and
Crankier, a
Grosser
Magic

The Book of Lancelot

1

Ahmed (another Ahmed)
All the ammo in all the mosques in Britain could not pay for the
  warmth of this shawarma
Lancelot took a chance, opened and closed the overhead
  storage cabinets, opened and closed, searching
Sancho, stomp it out on your eyeball
Agreeable? Say
Hello to my little
Friend
Willing to pay for that shawarma with anything
Civilized disobedience more holey
Than all the mosques in Britain
And less needy

2

Walking into the water after a kosher lamb burger the belch
  of the gulch of the dead sea
"It's all about the music"
Soldiers, sanctimoniously hummering into heaven
Dogpaddling desert. Terror as
Substantive as coliform
Count. Something stinks
In the sand. This war
Is the Trojan war. Is every war. A
Bloody trade war
"It's all about the music"
Waves of sound, simpler times totally
Washed up
Walking into the water, the
Library on fire
"It's all about the music"
If you are done as
Dinner (a British lunch)
Let me use Wagner

3

L'étranger, keep your eye on the ball
It can mimitate anything or anybody
Even a tennis lesson or metaphor
Glenn has already gotten started
Lancelot charged at the reading
Lancelot charged at the potluck
Lancelot charged at the big game
And slept with the symposium of
Self. "I'll never play again"
Missed the cup, Lancelot
His eyes so filled with
Tears

4

Love cannot exist between bounders
Trial versions. How fated the whole thing is
It is as if that desert were finally described
And the mirage slaked our thirst. With wet
You do know Graham how we love you and you love us
But nothing can stop the roar of the tide. The grail, not there
    becomes a light which is not able to be there like a
    lighthouse or spindrift
And remind Shannon to try The Fiddlehead
And remind Emily to try Dandelion
And remind Mariner to try Prism
And remind Moragh to try Opium
No, Graham, none of us can stop the pulse and beat of it
The roar

5

Lancelot borrowed the family
Clunker and committed sacrilege
But was enchanted elsewhere
To an undemanding lack
Of strings
Lancelot feared the question "where the fuck is my grail
    homes?" which nobody asked him
When the Shostakovich started
It was
For a time
His question to answer

6

The Germans have only invented seven useful things:
The three Bs, Mozart, Wagner
Leather shorts and
Lebensmittelgeschäft
(The longest word that Leaf learned)
Lancelot did not feel the need to
Prove leather shorts and the
Rest existed. They lived
Seriously, Garry is very much like entering
Music through the backdoor
Word, another trap
Door like rubbery gloved customs
Or leather shorts
Little place for Lancelot, who has
Crossed more borders
Than we are bored
Then, at the first post
War production of *Parsifal*, the
Overture began and
Lancelot coughed

7

He has all the sense of fun of persimmon. Complete
    and total persimmon
His sense of good and bad form is the sun (according to David Lean)
The morse he leads to water is not in love with the smell of
    camel (Herodotus). He frees the entrance of every
    servant and listens for the hollow resonance
He frees the entrance of every servant
"It's all about the music"
He repeats this mantra, music from an alpine goat
The Grail will not be his
Obviously

The Book of Gwenivere

1

Lance, where do we stand
On the edge of some suburban torment nowhere
    near the ocean nowhere near the beach
Lance, you gotta give me one more chance
The rainy coast is a lie I have left
Behind. The rainy coast is all wet. What
    do avian studies have to do
    with the price of frozen omelets
    in a California supermarket. Music
And magical transportation. What
Does it have I don't? Lady
Of the Lake I hate you
And those interesting girls
Who wear black. Listen
Lance, you gotta give me one more chance
I heard it at the mall

2

No. You never would have invited me
    into the grail castle. I am sure
You are there with all your pals
Right now. I am going to
Phone. Busy
I am sick of presence of absence
I am so old my life is over
Busy. Are you busy with
That bitch? O
Lance, do you remember
That time in the field
Under the moon
Our sand castle
Sans grail
Sand in your
Ass

3

Gung Haggis Fat Choy. They are celebrating
Are you still fasting? The
Alcoholic cherry was the
Beginning of your quest
Prints turned into road
You listen to him
Honestly you do
And I refuse to
Print him ever
You listen to him
Like a broken cup
And we contend
For your attention
Pointlessly, with
Cheap as chips
Nails. And then you are
Lifted from your earthly
Faith right into the Sky
Bar
        i was talking to you

4

What you don't understand. ie) You make
Love like a water flea. Lance, why do I
Love a water flea more than me. It
Is something I heard on my
Favourite show it was life
But you are always off
Grail-gathering. You said
You are going to do this
You are going to do that
You have done neither
You are worse than the
Moon I am jealous of
You say I love you

More than you love
Me. You are a water
Flea in the moon
Swimming

5

Sometimes I wonder what you are looking for
You used to call me your Angel
Visible. Available
You have flaked out on us
You have betrayed everything
For a vacant table and a side of
grail

6

Ancestral august ghosts
Where do we stand? Should
I throw in the matching towels
Lance, they do not know where
The grail castle will appear
In Egypt or Montréal. Damn
The ghosts and mystical lure
and the music I cannot hear
spirits that give you
Tourism
Naked
I lie in my room. The plums
Forget their significance
Hello, are you there?
Lance, if you're going to drink
That, then I want a
Sip

7

Proffered plums. For everyone. You are so
Polite, Lance. Enough to give both of us
Migraine. Hold on,   I
Have another call

I am empty, Lance
Empty as a stupid cup

I think I tried the grail
Maybe once upon a time
And it was very bitter

And I feel old, Lance
Like Veronica Mars
Too old to solve
Any more riddles

I am old as my father's plum tree
In the backyard. I remember one
Sunday he cut it down

Politely, your body woke me up
And I saw the bent morning

The Book of Merlin

1

Answer. Answer, damn you. In the
Warm of a question, weary of questing
Who will win the next imaginary turf
War? I must have perished perilous
Of curry sitting in the food court
I awoke with a different look
Get out of this business. No, I am
Bovine backbone in the desert
The repetition of hungry rats
That gnaw the shoes. Your
Magic will be better than their magic. You await that time with
    hunger
Strife
Is the thing only you can lift, enchanted healing
Gauntlet gone. And did anyone think to look for
Me? I was downtown the entire time
I told you so

2

For time immemorial
The river upheld the highest level of
Toxicity
And I have straggled into your midst
Like a converted Nostradamus
The lucid sky and mind barely able to hold
The drift of animals, the flight of flocks
Do you want to see my penis? This
Is the flash of knife, and outcast
Of a covenant. Into a grail cup
That is the history of Britain
There is always a prophecy
At the end of time. There
Is always the end of time

3

The cave locked behind him
Like some party closet game
He could see through time
And stubborn grime behind
The refrigerator. But
Love was opaque
A slug-proof vest to the
Chambers of his eyes
Packing. A bird
Could flap through a hole of
Flesh without hitting a single
Grail
Love persisted
With starched bastards
And stiff calumny

4

Otherwise everything was brilliant
Peachy as punch. Love was made
Under the fireworks. Love was
Bottle rocket released inside
As if the disenfranchised could
Never know it, had not shared it
From the innards of his cave
Merlin watched
The entire exhibition
And it was so much hotter
With a flag over your face

5

I am the soft-boiled political
Prisoner in a cruel state of mind
She said I was the loneliest thing
She who led me into the dank dark
Of her own loneliness. She
Had missed the point
She who locked me in and
Insisted she had been locked
Out. She had wanted to raise the price
Of boredom and short-sell the
Strategy of patience. I have
Learned a lack of boredom
There was a Grail but she did not know that
Stewing outside

6

Hither and thither, mark
Let the East narrow their real
Estate and perceptions and
Covet the last standing tree
And let the West pop open
Whorish legs laced in smog
The song of too much forest
And the Lady of the Lake
With her literal palmjobs
Because the people want
More palmjobs and less
Labour. Fine. Go on strike
It plays no part in the magic
It poisons a palmful of trees
Utter my name(s). I am Merlin
    penned in a limb of the Grail Castle

7

"Se non tollari il calore"
Weite Speicher der Kraft schafft sich der
Zeitgeist, gestaltlos
Can you hear the tone of the ring
Tonight birds chirping
Can you hear the tone of the ring
It is the special phone
Reality is calling you for help
Enshrouded in autumn fog
A red-winged blackbird
Answers
The typing of the tone of the ring
Whad'ya want? The table is not even
Round, and wobbles back and forth
There will be no more poetry, forever
Unless
Unless
You part and play your part and do your part
And locate some naked legs for this table
That is my prophecy, ad absurdum
Because the first minute is free

The Book of Gal

1

Born in tinders, a glam of Euro
Wood, she believed in the
Forest so strongly she
Kissed her pet wolf farewell
And trotted into town
(Ideal city)
Dressed as a boy
Her armour harder and more
Heavenly than any hazy
Paramour
Through the horror
Massacres and moons
She bid the hooves clip
By the night she sped
Back, she and all the
Wood were
                              moved
Not a tree in
Vision. All invisible or
Never was. And they
Did not get her holy
Forest marked by
Imaginary wolves

2

Boy
She said to an entourage of in
Distinct saplings
The Grail is sure heavy
Her eyes were tired
Encrusted like the cup
From lack of use
Because the grail
Is very bright
Boy

The Grail is sure heavy
I hope for more bling
In this ringing copse
In these singing cups
The Grail is sure heavy
You fucking cops
But the O.P.P.
Went to bed
Without a sniff
Without a whiff
Without
Luminosity

3

She was the coolest
Knight in deconstructed
Duds to find the cup
She was secretly
Cherished by an
Entire decade of
Magic. The news
Reported her missing. An
Entire decade of
Tragic. Go
West, the
Voices admired
And endure the
Rest

4

Whispers
Fading celebration
Fashionable
Lateness
Whispers
Left
Over wine
Hunks of brie
Galahad, ghost child
Of transparent cognac
In diminutive
Grail glass
Whispers
A book that stays open
Talk about a table
One
Hermes, green
One purple wall
Allowable
Whispers

5

After the initial shock, they
Suggested corrections to the
Purity of Galahad. All the
Greatest Knights of the
Realm and their sponsors
Pour paint thinner into
Her transparent cup
Chemical fare, the
Fatigue of the realm
She had forgotten in all the
Gleam
To wear her bulletproof
Speech and war

Paint
Sparkling and acidulous
They said you
Missed a
Spot

6

The Grail was a statement
Cooked up to sit upon
Stomach, inoffensively

The Grail was a kosher
Serving that time we
Split an animal

The Grail is the sun
Except something else
Less harmful to vision

The Grail is the moon
Too preoccupied to be
Observed drinking

The Grail would repair
Senses of irresponsibility
And fix my broken train

7

Dear sir
S/he wrote the wood
Is hersir or sirher more
Appropriate
Appropriate
Appropriate
Except it sounded more like
Finnegan waking
Chop chop chop

Derelynge, I have to tell you
In the biggest pink
Ear of the forest
The grail is not
Wearing squat
And the wordiness
Of the woodiness
Shrunk her down to
Size of a pine needle
With no place to go
For a new grail bag
Vienna, maybe

The Book of the Return of Arthur

1

“Wish we knew
How t’quit you”
One more time in Provençal
Cold blue mercenary tune
Check the obvious
Symbolism at the unsavoury
Check. Written in tire
Tracks, homoerotic Kerouac
Come back. Check. This is a
Perfect paper. Beats and beats
Like pie and ice cream (S-E-X)
Stuck in a gleaming ice cube
In the gullet all that cool talk
“Nebraska I ain’t got no use for”
I am king
Of a tapioca basement
Of every parent’s worst
Dreaming of formica
Open

2

The acne of Jessica Simpson attacked by a truth serum
In the Mall of America
“I didn’t get
Where I am
Without flaws”
I don’t work there anymore
Our quid-pro-quo always the same. Only a king
    on a milk carton can suck the rampant pus
    of the celebrated. Or auction their bling
He took her life. Like Nirvana first sounding like the
Beatles in another poem. He left her
Barren as Barnes and Noble
In the Mall of America
Come back, O king

Come back with her
Dead underwear

3

The eternal night before the grail hunt, no
Body could get a wink, especially the king
He tied the silk token around his headache
And bid his favourite pair good eve
Save Galahad, who was blessed by
Placecards and musical chairs and
Hopped into the sack of his liege
For one last hurrah before
Purity could fire
A starting pistil. Itself
The grail was a lonely hunt. Often
Snowed in
Without the comfort of gushing
Crusades or the solace of no
Sin inns. And the lack of
Sodomy was
Palpable
Sinking into the depths
Of his adjustable chair
Arthur wept
And waited like Water
Gate for the symbolic
Mug to smart
His pagan smirk
Naturally, it was a dis
Appointment

4

A far off
Drink in the Ivanhoe for a century
Faint call in the distance, the reverb of
Warping nintendo. There was

Nothing to do that night
But play chess solitaire
Under the table. This poem, verily
Every poem is this poem
Depends upon that fault. And she
Looked too much like Sylvia Plath
Whining to be Gwenivere. She
Didn't want to watch the game. She
Wanted to smoke and smoke. Mean
While you were St. Elsewhy
Exposed upon the mullet of time
With all particulars created
Equal, along with Jessica
Simpson's sexy acne
Reborn, made in the us
Immortali(s)ered
Hey Meeeeeeeeeeegan
What a drag

5

Sangrin, I have forgotten why the sankgreal
Was so freaking hot. It fell off the back of a
Galloping morse or some shit. Ask
Lancelot. If you ask, he can get you anything
Books, tickets, blow. Just ask
Minnesota Viking, ware ye not forget the
Ancient charm, Norwegian whispers
Along the seawall and nothing else
Learned in Africa or some shit
Ware ye not, Merlin is
Opening his robes and
Spreading likely stories
Come back to us, rey
Americano. Let go of that eternal
Celtic Monkees rendition. And snow. And
Remember, Target, then Krögers
And then the duty
Free shop

6

C: Drive, you knew how to
Downsize your inferior superior
Down to size. And became
King. And we loved you for it
Power hungry americano. You
Could not build a wall big enuff
To spell check yourself from
Our heart or liver conditions
If this crazy glue of a world
Was to include love, we
Wanted you to watch. And
We could feel your beard
Bristle with beckoning all the way
Down to the brickhouse. And you
Were most judicious when Bartosz
Could not hear the animals. And you
Erected a gargantuan sculpture of your
Beard and spelled it C-U-N-T. And
This is a mimetic sculpture
Of exactly what
Happens

7

Memories, stuck in head like crumbs in over
Grown beard. They teach us these days
Nostalgia is dangerous. I know the
Knight of the Smile is no longer
Smiling is deep in Cerveza is
Behind a wall in Mexico. Come
Back and come upon the cross
Where you left us hanging. We
Cannot see the books for the trees
Nor quite hear the echo of cunts
"I'm hip to time"
This is an essay for your eternal

Birthday in a fireant kitchen
Wilt thou ne'er return to
hear it
Arthur, king and spiked earl
Grey. Dear hersir, come back to the all
Thing and assume your thirsty
Booth
This is stuck in the head. Something like
Your nintendo riff. Shave for chrissake
And nab the next greyhound. In
Spite of all this morseshit, this
Uncomfortable muzak

Letters West

1

The planet Gatineau (Hull) has its own rules and way of doing things and meeting its own ends. The bridges are impeccable for burning. But try catching a bus and you will discover the system is different. The planet is sometimes even pretty on a cloudless night

I can see you in the distance. I can

The talk is being talked at one about winter whiter and colder than the blankest of pages. The talk freezes midair and forms words in the shape of icicles. The talk is festive and frightens those who are unable

Gatineau (Hull) is its own industry that manufactures positions that rarely orbit. It consists of blocks and blocks of weeping buildings. Historically imagination was a chief export

The birds are the same but sing in a different pidgin. They are carrier birds and masters of encoded transmission. They sing the same message of love for their planet and no other planet. At night they disguise themselves as bureaucrats in a balsamic sky. No one studies closely

Gatineau (Hull) has two moons and neither knows what the other is doing
On a cloudless night each collision is covered by a cold white page

Come home. Come home. This is merely transmission failure. This is translation failure. The birds never sing things like that

There is providence in a cold bird finding a turd

You are right. It is snowing

Love,
Garry

2

When you talked across the Outaouais the bulbous streetlamps bulged and glowed with afterthoughts. When you talked across the Outaouais smiling beasts revived from extinction and sunlight flooded a giant blotter in front of the window

Old desires do not fade or leave. They are accidentally dropped into new land one might yet till. The roots stir and munificent plants and animals emerge But they cannot feed you. Ask your nearest neighbour

When you knelt beside me and drank from the river of vowels my eyes brimmed over

Love is not enough. One has to ratify it for fear of acting a Romantic. Our tentative contract must endure the most stubborn and chilling of winds

> SEEK LONELINESS IN NUMBERS
> BECOME ANOTHER
> HOLD ABSURD VIGIL
> EXPECT NOTHING
> SEEK HELP IN THE SURPRISING

When I finally thought of something funny or slightly off and turned you were no longer there. This life is an open book, an open letter that is the craftiest of all, lived heartily in the camouflage of plain sight

The clearing felt empty without you

I have reached the precise bifurcation where people and places and poems are interchangeable and ready to be exchanged. I reserve wishes and maledictions for the ever flowing river of vowels. I recall how much you dislike poems being mentioned in poems and shrug helplessly

I have dragged the heart-shaped kite this far, hoping for a sudden gust of enthusiasm. A sudden paroxysm of pleasure. This is each moment for me behind the painted canvas of my person, a ripe possibility dancing upon the end of a line of twine

Maybe we have no faith, and that is to say refusing to put our breath into it where the tremulous organ beats most wildly. This breathing exercise is the only faith required and has enough magic to lift a thousand flagging poems

This is elusive as any bell

This is real as a V of birds

Love,
Garry

3

There are surface images we affix to what cannot be expressed, to shocks and disappointments and cries for help and a modicum of solace. These images are mutable yet retain the same symbolic currency. They are permanent stamps for eternity

A bell, a bird, a lost coin in the lane, a smile, a shadow, a small wave. These are what I have tried to exchange for human love. I did not know what it was. I turned away and ran after the wrong picture that was disconnected from perhaps one source of happiness

I recall wintry bus shelters and a mouth full of freshly picked cherries. I recall the souls of dogs. I recall closeness unlike any other

I am scarcely more than a permanent stamp affixed to another letter on its way to you, clinging to this frail semblance of a self forgotten or more recently disinterred

On account of this peculiarity all sense of time is lost. Two moons apart is a heartrending lifetime where the message never arrives on time. Yet in life even tragedy misses its cue, is imperfect. We continue to live without dramatic imperative

However permanent there is price and heft. Even the freest of spirits has to scrounge for even one permanent stamp of the heart. At last one can let go of all of Montaigne

Send for me. That is all I need to hear. Beyond the lively trade of plane and rail and bus tickets send for me. Send for me if only to suffer the expense of one permanent stamp, first class

Love,
Garry

4

All the weeping in the world cannot change the colour of the green room or erode the old stone walls of Vieux-Québec. I have bitten out my spleen and left it for the waters of the Kahnawake to swallow

Consolation is being reunited with a manic brilliant mind for another fleeting moment since we are always ghosts just missing one another. Nor can I unsing the apparition I left in that little upstairs room

I have had to reinvent the entire city in such a short interim. I have had to renovate every road and streetlamp to cast the exact amount of surreality, to mark your passage

The art of divestment is a worthy one with the merits of any trade school. For the first night I know what it is to sleep like that fellow with the bells against an unmurdered maple. I plant my own tree where convenient

Walk with me and I will recount all the tears upon all the old stones of Vieux-Québec. Talk with me and I will recount everything the walls of the green room taught me. The invisible

We are better off this way, better off than Odysseus' dog

Love,
Garry

5

Imagine living life to gust up a few lines upon a page. When sending for me with all of one's heart is not enough to shift a few words from point O to V

Lives atrophy and tear at their mourning fabric. But the babbling persists, the multitude of voices in this lonely place. This solitary joy during interminable delays is lost on literary personalities and ramble to a logy audience. Life is here between torn meal-tickets where delays are impetus

There is no point in running off to wipe spilt coffee from these letters. There is no point in hoarding something for someone else. The waiting room is frightful. It enchants and entices and entraps and ultimately kills to know of

The chatter in the dwindling lounge is not enough to drown the silence of poetry. It makes no sense to interrupt the nearest braggart to point out the most trampled and demolished of lives gave an arbitrary arrangement of words a disembodied voice

Even to write would be interference. Staticky lips can move all by themselves Talking noggins prime for stuffing. What can I say but every waking moment I missed this necessary loneliness

The hurt is a learning, even for lips that have forgotten how to kiss

Love,
Garry

6

I nibble your notes and make profound interpretations of them. What is not a form of augury

I have hidden this form of longing that has no solid target and is not quite reaching for person, place or thing

I sang some Russian opera the other night and thought I got the tone of the thing. I was utterly sincere and in the same breath in a fugue. The aesthetic surface should strip away like salami covering yet it lingers to the point of imitating food

George Stanley thought Garreth Tintern Moss was *hyperelegant.* It's like Lavery dropping by with his butter and his crusts and his terminology for the way I write. The condensation of terms like *onslaughterer* linger upon abandoned windows

I am returning to spring and rain and fog and shiny new trains. I am returning under a layer of exquisite ignominy. I am returning to bright hues and the tuberlike promise of regeneration

In such a spring the lieder are sincere. The sound of love pains really sounds like *Liebesschmertz* and this compounds one's problems. The hurt was necessary for innumerable hearts to spring open

I wish to sleep and feel you cover me like a moss the shade of paper. I wish to unavert my face

Love,
Garry

7

You are more vivid the less objects I have to remind me of frozen time. This leaves me hopeful, as if it were the finest trick to at last escape this daisy chain of airports. You are more here anyway where I am barely visible

I have one permanent stamp left and it contains an entire dead letter office. I have switched to the right currency now and all the horses have been sold or left behind to nostril the waft of chlorine

I hang around like a favourite mug and try to avoid the chicanery of faux-Delftware. And the words pour into me with their own means of manifestation. They bear the heft of prophetic relation to objects in the real world while I enjoy forgetfulness after a good rinse

That is to say I feel vitally alive when this substance is flowing through me even if it is only a division of cheesecloth. I feel the fakery has been life up to the very nub of this transmission. No one has been able to see the way my trembling knees make the table move

The post office is nearly closed. I recall someone asking for it in the middle of the night

Love,
Garry

8

This letter is from the other Garry, the treacherous nervous creature who stuffs letters into envelopes and then scarcely recollects them upon waking

He has been accused of going into fugues. The question is whether they have interrupted a new life or whether a new life has been one prolonged fugue. Now we are enjoying a familiar beloved theme upon the ghostly radio in the kitchen Sometimes I can even hear that noisy needy goldfish tossing rocks about

Although he tried so dutifully to scratch away all traces of ancillary life, it has reared its head to supplant what was just happening, leaving it like the briefest skip in a record or briefest skip of pebble across choppy waves

On the other side is a musical butterfly unless it is only a reflection. In spite of dragging that *daimon* around, he is once in a butane moon radiant

Love (and listen)
Garry

9

The antique vanity continues to exist without its mirror. Some nights, I can hear its namesake breaking. It is too much of a solid lesson to serve as anything functional

The vanity is another reason for not writing because there are no ideal circumstances for the arrival of a poem or letter. Reaching for even one object damages the hands

The letters must learn to rise to the occasion of themselves. They are just catching their breath and gaining momentum. The letters whisper behind our backs and imply a mirror where there is none

They persist like inexplicable impromptus

The vanity loiters, yet lacks the lure of kitchen stories and the intimacy of a bed

Love,
Garry

10

Please overlook the letters riddled with riddles. I cannot even hear their content over the roaring wave of the karaoke machine. I could not have said what needed to get said

I have had to learn that people look and act like other people. They evaporate into clouds and then suddenly imbue crowds with glints of recognition. One time I hugged you so fiercely, mistaking you for someone else. Our bel canto technique is crammed with cant, slipping loose from essentials

In spite of all my admonitions about heading East and scattering one's localism I was a perfect hypocrite in doing so myself. This is something about poetry and it knows it

There is safety in numbers behind every superficial hug and wave and incomprehensible construct. I prefer the immediacy of igniting bridges I am just about to recline under

When there is finally time, let us not squander its overstimulated ticks. Days blender into years so easily. Like your voice between the ears. Like letters in the sun

Love,
Garry

11

To whom it may concern I sincerely hope to touch. We drop and slide and glide our voices at the drop of a that. To whom am I divining which

There is room for a hint of religion in the pound shop in Carlingwood Mall There are old-fashioned benches and the festive interior must have saved countless lives from economic depression, where an old man has time to try imported water and an old woman can order liver and onions in a hurry

You crave particulars but is that how you divined the future? Was it more clarified than very good butter or a shriek or a squeak? I could even see your lovely mouth moving. I felt you beside me and this was sufficient for my febrile nerves

Shall I dispatch my doppelgänger to catch up with yours, to force a door of that mutual fragility? I am able to wait for years upon this foghorned coast for beauty to once again wash ashore, the reversal of every myth. Holding vigil is my superlative craft and to quote a Nordic proverb, *dreams don't mean anything*

This is not important to a magus who jongleurs semantics at the drop of a that This is not important when the mouth is full of Lebanese meat pie. My significant other would tell yours to buy a calendar marked down and to mark the days

I never let his sound in at four in the morning. But you never knocked

Garry

12

I have no doubt these letters should have been penned and postscribed. I have no doubt these letters should subsist on what fleeting attention they might attract. But whether they should be read at a reading to punctuate their already flagging hearts. That would be ostentatious as announcing disposable graffiti under bridges, like a love affair you tell everyone about

Magic freezes blood. Like the cue a card might divine for the throat or the antique creatures made manifest in the gentle revelation of a letter. I talk to you the way I would talk all night, in order to filch for myself the fire of an improper visit. To find you at the interstice of mangled form and incoherent content

The opposite is poetry or pajamas or pregnant pauses or Proust or anything difficult in the universe that begins with P

It's all done with magnets and mirrors and smoke inhalation. I could speak of the melodramatic theatrics of my people but I won't. I could evoke rational ties to the land but I won't. There is an arbitrariness to forcing letters into alphabets. There is agony in the metonymy of the head of a heard

This is so close to the truth I won't finish the letter

Love,
Garry

13

Messagio Galore was the most common phrase to parse, statistically speaking. I had only the footprints of a bird on the wet sand and the raised murmur of voices in the green room and the sudden hush keeping me up. I don't know what type of bird it was

There is a dusty old piece about a couple who cannot hear itself talk (or think) The questions raised into voices within it make no more nonsense than tarot divinations and tables knocked to and fro by trembling knees

There are pretty petty ironies in the way we keep missing one another. I thought to sing to you forever the chant of pictures and letters that blaze upon the wall. I thought to sing of secretive stencil patterns in the quirkiest of corners. I thought to charge you like a rutting quark

Messagio Galore is the most universal public address message from OUTSIDE
I overheard it in the Men's

I give you back to that long-winded wild

Love,
Garry

14

In the Time Capsule a permanent stamp would suffice to mark the occasion. It would live longer than overpriced animate stamps

No one knows better than I do how lonely

In the Time Capsule there are the most complicated relationships and the most intricate systems of horse trading. The immobile greats stare directly ahead and sell their butter right and left over the smell of chlorine. And all afternoon, the Jack Purcell Centre is the centre of the universe

Live longer than living stamps. Live longer, damn you

In the Time Capsule the time mechanics are all on strike. Meanwhile, they argue about making peace. The encoded logic lining the walls, combined with the überweak coffee, convinced me to buy one stamp that might outlive all others

The permanent stamp has a picture of the Time Capsule upon it; I have taken three capsules already, and one for the journey

No one knows how lonely